West Mo

THE HISTORY OF THE
WEST MONMOUTHSHIRE OMNIBUS BOARD
1926-74

Michael Yelton
and
Chris Taylor

WEST MONMOUTHSHIRE
OMNIBUS BOARD

BEDWELLTY AND MYNYDDISLWYN URBAN DISTRICT COUNCILS

R.T. BROWN, M.B.E., J.P., A.M. INST.T.
GENERAL MANAGER.

ISBN 978 1905 304 264

Computer Origination, Design and Layout by John A Senior

Contents

Photographic Credits

Chris Taylor collection	CTC
Michael Yelton collection	MYC
Geoff Lumb	GL
Roy Marshall	RM
British Commercial Vehicle Museum/Leyland Motors	BCVM
Senior Transport Archive	STA

Please note that all pictures in appendix 2 have come from Chris Taylor's collection.

Front cover illustration: The first post-war 8ft wide vehicles, a pair of all Leyland PD2/12s, entered service in 1953. Originally they were painted with cream window frames, later being repainted in the 3-band livery as seen here. Subsequently the lower cream band was brought round under the front cab window. LWO 322 (No. 8) was withdrawn in the summer of 1968. (*CTC*)

Rear cover illustration: The last new double-decker delivered to the Board arrived in 1966. It was repainted into the new livery in May 1970 with more blue than had been applied to the previous repaints, which then became the standard. KWO 134D (No. 28) passed to Islwyn Borough Transport in 1974. (*GL*)

Introduction

For reasons which are not clear, far less has been written on the history of buses in Wales than in other parts of the United Kingdom, and virtually nothing has been put together on the small but distinctive valley local authority fleets. Of these the most charismatic, and nowadays for enthusiasts of a certain age the most evocative, was the West Monmouthshire Omnibus Board. The fame of the Board largely arose from its operations on the fearsome Bargoed Hill, for which special vehicles were bought and which required great expertise from the drivers on it. The Board had an unusual legal basis and struggled throughout to cope with poor roads, extremely difficult operating conditions and an inability to take over the more lucrative interurban services. This book endeavours to show its history in the light of all these factors. We are indebted to all who have assisted, especially Glyn Coleman, the last General Manager of the Board, who enabled the text to be much enlightened by his reminiscences of a lifetime working for West Mon. Sadly he died before the book was published. We are also grateful to the PSV Circle and Omnibus Society for their extensive research into the fleet history of the Board, published as long ago as 1974, on which we have drawn for much information. Finally, our thanks are due to Venture Publications for their enthusiasm for and support with the project.

Chris Taylor
Michael Yelton

October 2008

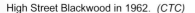

High Street Blackwood in 1962. *(CTC)*

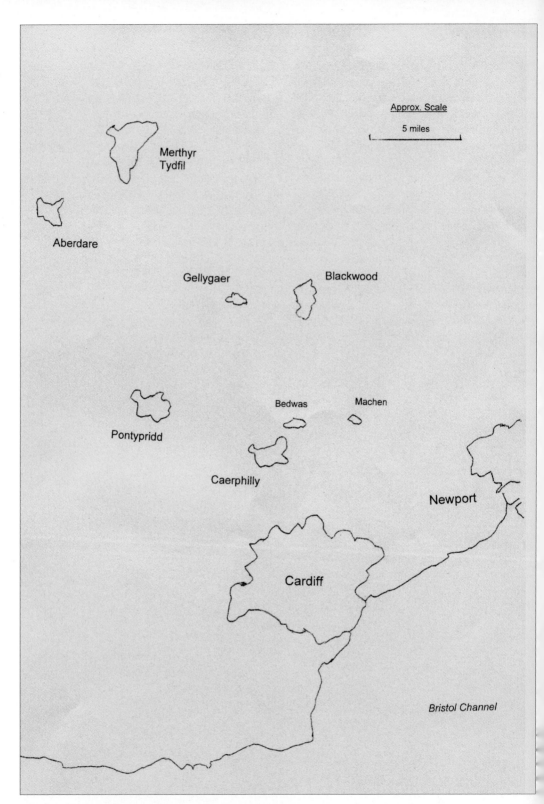

Approx. Scale

5 miles

Merthyr
Tydfil

Aberdare

Gellygaer

Blackwood

Pontypridd

Bedwas

Machen

Caerphilly

Newport

Cardiff

Bristol Channel

This map of South Wales shows the location of all the former municipal operators in the area and in particular the proximity of the valleys operators.

Chapter One

FORMATION

Part VIII of the Mynyddislwyn Urban District Council Act 1926 may appear a strange starting point for a book on buses, but it was by virtue of that part of that Act that the West Monmouthshire Omnibus Board, familiarly known as 'West Mon' from the fleetname carried for many years, was incorporated. In fact section 62(1) reads specifically: 'A board (to be called "the West Monmouthshire Omnibus Board") shall be established for the purpose of providing and running omnibuses…'

The Board was not strictly speaking a municipal operator, although usually categorised as such, because it was a body corporate in its own right, with its own coat of arms. However, the Act provided that it should initially have nine members, six appointed by Bedwellty UDC and three by Mynyddislwyn, and these numbers remained unaltered throughout. In other words it was clearly and directly under local authority control and in many respects was equated legally with a more conventional civic transport organisation, but on the other hand was not directly answerable to all the councillors in the way in which were other municipal transport departments.

Before looking further at the formation of the Board and then at its operation, it may be helpful to look at the topography and background of the area which the Board served. The historic boundary between Glamorganshire and Monmouthshire ran down the Rhymney river. Caerphilly and Gelligaer (originally Gellygaer) UDCs, both bus operators, were just on the Glamorgan side: Bedwas & Machen, for many years the smallest municipal fleet, was just on the Monmouthshire side. The two urban districts of Bedwellty and Mynyddislwyn were also just on the Monmouthshire side, and both were named after small hill villages rather than the surrounding industrial towns which had grown up in the Nineteenth Century: Gelligaer was in a similar situation as the largest town within that district was Bargoed. The largest settlement in the Bedwellty area was the town of Blackwood, which was to be the centre of the Board's operations throughout, although the Council Offices were further up the valley at Aberbargoed. The largest township in

Mynyddislwyn was Pontllanfraith, just south of Blackwood, which also housed the administration of the Council, and indeed the village after which the area was named was never itself served by the Board or by any other buses, despite proposals from time to time. The boundaries are not entirely logical, and the Maes-y-Cwmmer district, which lies between Blackwood and the important interchange point at Ystrad Mynach just on the Glamorganshire side of the river, was in fact in Bedwas & Machen Urban District, although some distance from those townships and connected to them only by a very narrow road.

The area is typical of the South Wales valley towns, with steep gradients, and roads and railways usually following the rivers; at the time of the Board's operations there were many working coal mines. It was a region which in the interwar period was the scene of much poverty, and there was little money to spend on leisure activities. The year in which the Board was established was also the year of the General Strike, which coincided with a much longer strike by miners. However, in the period before the economic depression of the 1930s, there was a considerable amount of new building in the area: the local architect AF Webb of Blackwood designed the mining village of Oakdale in 1909-10 on Garden City principles, and he was responsible in the late 1920s for the new cul-de-sac village of Wyllie and the estate at Penllwyn, both in Pontllanfraith.

Bus operation in the area was extremely difficult. Although loads at certain times were very high, the roads were poor and liable to subsidence and landslip. The Board is best known for its operation on the fearsome Bargoed Hill, but there were many other steep gradients on the system, which meant that the winter brought particular problems in its wake. The direct road between New Tredegar and Abertysswg, now completely closed by landslips, provided other problems in operation.

The area has of course a very strong tradition of adherence to the Labour Party, and municipal operation was regarded by many as a proper reflection of those political views rather than as a business proposition: indeed the well-known politician Aneurin Bevan was for a time the chairman of the Monmouthshire Bus Licensing Committee. There was especial resentment at the idea that local bus services should be provided from outside the area. Of the smaller valley towns, Aberdare and Pontypridd both ran trams and trolleybuses and began motor bus operation in 1924 and 1930 respectively. Caerphilly also commenced running motor buses in 1920, Bedwas & Machen in 1922, West Mon in 1926 and Gelligaer in 1928: none of this latter group had run electric transport.

The intention to begin local municipal operation in the Board's area was signalled in a private bill introduced by Bedwellty in 1923, which was opposed by the existing operators and was lost at the committee stage: Bedwellty then joined forces with Mynyddislwyn, which was promoting another a bill of its own to give itself enhanced powers in other spheres, and Part VIII, setting up the Board, was tacked on to that. Mynyddislwyn itself had tried once before, in 1916, but that attempt had been unsuccessful.

The provisions of the Act of 1926 are extremely detailed, and they include, in the Second Schedule, two agreements made with the respective Councils on behalf of the as then unincorporated Board, both dated 7th June 1926, one of which was made with Lewis & James Ltd, and the other with Griffin Motor Company Ltd, the Valleys Motor Bus Services Ltd, and Western Services Ltd, by which these operators withdrew their opposition to the Bill in consideration of the Board buying certain premises and vehicles.

The main Act gave the Board power to run buses (a) within the districts of the two Councils, and (b), with the consent of the Minister of Transport and of the relevant other local authority, in any district adjoining Mynyddislwyn Urban District, in any part of Caerphilly Urban District within two miles of Mynyddislwyn UD, and between New Tredegar and Abertysswg in the area of Rhymney UD. These restrictions on running out of the area were of relatively short duration, because under the Road Traffic Act 1930 any local authority (which was defined by s108(1) to include a Joint Board such as West Mon) which was already operating was authorised to run within its area or, with the consent of the Traffic Commissioners, outside it.

The Board, as is apparent from the agreements scheduled to the Act, began its operations not from scratch but rather by taking over and developing existing services owned by the company operators.

Lewis & James began operations as a motor garage in Newbridge in 1919 and then in June 1921 began running buses from Crumlin to Newport, using the trading name Western Valleys Garage & Engineering. The latter name was used to incorporate a new company in 1920. In October 1925 they took over the Blackwood-based Sirhowy Valley fleet and thereafter adopted the trading name 'Western and Sirhowy Valleys', which was also carried on the vehicles. A contemporary timetable shows the basic operation on routes operated by Lewis & James shortly before the incorporation of the Board as being:

1.	Crumlin-Newbridge-Abercarn-Newport.
2.	Ynysddu-Wattsville-Newport.
3.	Newbridge-Pontllanfraith-Blackwood-Pengam-Bargoed-Deri.
4.	Ystrad Mynach-Pengam-Bargoed.
5.	Blackwood-Pontllanfraith-Aberbargoed-New Tredegar-Abertysswg.
6.	Blackwood-Markham-Hollybush-Markham-Aberbargoed.
7.	Blackwood-Pontllanfraith-Oakdale.

The agreement provided for the transfer to the Board of all the 'interior routes', ie those running within the area of the two urban districts, plus extensions to Abertysswg and Pengam and 'the proposed extension of the Markham-Aberbargoed route to Bargoed' (the famous Bargoed Hill route), for which it is made clear elsewhere in the agreement that two special vehicles had been ordered. Thus services 5, 6 and 7 were transferred, together with the right to operate between Pontllanfraith and Pengam on service 3, and also a leasehold garage in Blackwood High Street, four Leyland 30-seat vehicles, one Daimler with 26 seats, and two Thornycrofts, one with 26 and one with 20 seats. The exact details of all these vehicles were not clear when the PSV Circle and Omnibus Society published their fleet history in 1974, but further research since that time has thrown much more light on the situation. Full known details of these and other vehicles later owned by the Board are set out in the detailed fleet list which follows this narrative. The acquired vehicles were in any event soon withdrawn.

The Board was also given the option after the expiry of ten years to purchase the through routes of the vendors together with vehicles and depots, but the option was lost if the business of Lewis & James had by then been acquired by any other operator. It is worth bearing in mind that at this time there were serious proposals from Risca and Abercarn UDCs to buy out the remainder of the Lewis & James business and to operate buses under the aegis of a Western Valleys Omnibus Board, but in the end these did not proceed because the ratepayers voted against the proposal in a local referendum in February 1927. Lewis & James then sold out in August 1927 to the National Electric Construction Company, which already owned the Rhondda Tramways Company. The relatively small consideration for this sale was £25,250, which suggests that the vendors' undertaking was not particularly profitable. In 1933 the former Lewis & James operations were absorbed into the new Western Welsh company.

The other three companies, with whom the second agreement in the Schedule to the 1926 Act was made, represented what became the Red & White strand in transport in South Wales. Griffin, run by SJ Jones and Guy Bown, began as a garage company in Brynmawr in 1919, and then started a bus service in 1921. It took its name from the company premises at Old Griffin Yard, from where horse buses had been run by the hotel of the same title. By 1924 they had begun running through from Ebbw Vale and Brynmawr to Blackwood via Crumlin and in December 1925 they took over the Blackwood (Monmouthshire) Motor Company

with local routes from Blackwood to Ystrad Mynach (via two routes), Ynysddu and Wattsville, and Oakdale, and a garage in Ystrad Mynach. Valleys (as opposed to 'Western Valleys') was a business started by JH Watts and some associates in Tredegar in 1921, although the operational headquarters was at Lydney. One of the first services was Tredegar-Hollybush-Markham-Blackwood-Pontllanfraith, and in the same year they acquired a service between Blackwood and Oakdale via Pontllanfraith run by WE Price. The directors of Griffin and of Valleys were friendly, and in 1925 they incorporated Western Services Ltd, with SR Jenkins, a well respected local non-party politician, who was a member of Abercarn UDC as well being on the Bus Licensing Committee and also a Magistrate, as the front man, although shortly afterwards directors were appointed from the two backing companies and in due course Jenkins left and set up on his own account. The purpose behind the company was to acquire licences from local authorities without being tarred by the brush of outsiders which

Sirhowy Valley Motor Transport was founded in 1919 and was taken over by Lewis & James' Western Valleys Company in 1925. A number of former Sirhowy Valley vehicles passed to the West Monmouthshire Omnibus Board on its establishment, although this Leyland was not one of them. *(CTC)*

inevitably attached particularly to the Watts family, who came from the Forest of Dean, but also to the Griffin partners. The business quickly developed a Tredegar to Newport service via Hollybush, Markham, Blackwood, Pontllanfraith, Ynysddu and Wattsville, which ran right through the urban districts of both Bedwellty and Mynyddislwyn. It then took over S Coombes of Oakdale and extended his Blackwood-Pontllanfraith-Oakdale service on to Crumlin and Pontypool. Western Services had an office in Blackwood: it is also interesting that it used a similar name to Western Valleys, and also ran vehicles in a blue livery, although darker than their rivals.

The agreement with the three companies was similar to that with Lewis & James, but there were significant detailed differences. Griffin and Valleys agreed to sell to the Board their own 'interior routes', which were defined for this purpose as those running wholly within the two urban districts and between either of them and Ystrad Mynach. Griffin therefore sold all the services which they had bought from the Blackwood (Mon) Motor Company Ltd, and Valleys sold the ex-Price service to Oakdale. The Western Services service through to Pontypool was not an 'interior route' and therefore remained with them. There were other provisions as to competition on various roads which necessitated Western Services being a party to the agreement, and in particular the companies agreed not to vary their own timetables on specified routes. The Board agreed to buy from Griffin a leasehold garage in Ystrad Mynach, two Dennis 32-seaters, one AEC, one Leyland and one Daimler, all with 26 seats, one Reo with 14 seats, and various stores including two Daimler char-a-bancs. From Valleys they took one Albion 22-seater, one Commer of unspecified capacity, and a petrol pump in Blackwood. There are still odd aspects of this transaction: it seems that the char-a-bancs were never operated, but even more curiously the Commer was said to have been towed down to Blackwood from the premises of Hills in Tredegar. It never ran for the Board.

The provisions relating to the option to acquire external services were not identical to those in the Lewis & James agreement. The Board was given an option to require any of the three other parties to sell them their through services and related vehicles and premises: there was no exclusion of that option if the other companies had sold on the services, as there was in the case

A more modern vehicle in the Sirhowy Valley fleet was this Thornycroft A1 with a body believed to be built by J Norman. An ex-Sirhowy Thornycroft become No. 7 in the West Mon fleet. *(CTC)*

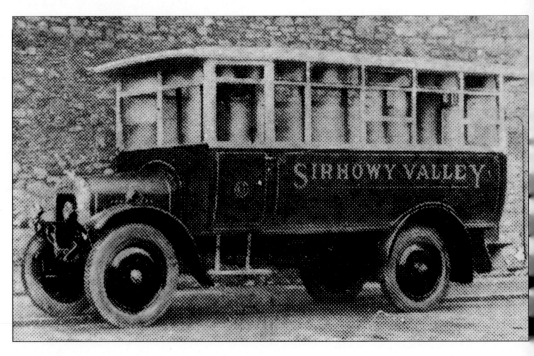

of Lewis & James. Valleys and Western Services' assets were purchased by Red & White Services Ltd in an amalgamation dated 1st January 1930, and Griffin's directors became directors of Red & White Services Ltd. However both Griffin itself and Ralph's Garages Ltd of Abertillery were not absorbed by Red & White: they became subsidiaries of a new company, Griffin Ralph Ltd, in which Red & White had only a minority shareholding. It appears that this labyrinthine structure may partly have been devised for financial reasons, but partly also to ensure the predominance of the Watts family interests in the main Red & White business. In 1950 of course the directors of Red & White United Transport Ltd, which was formed in 1937 as a parent company for the entire group, sold their English and Welsh bus operations to the BTC.

The Act received Royal Assent on 4th August 1926 and the Board began operations in October of that year with the routes set out above and the vehicles inherited from the other companies. The effect of the agreements was to burden the new Board with very considerable debt. It paid £7000 to Lewis & James, £7524 to Griffin and £1275/8/6d to Valleys, which were large sums for the time: in addition it agreed that if it established the Bargoed Hill route it would buy the two vehicles ordered for it by Lewis & James. The vehicles acquired were not only assorted, but in some cases of poor quality, and the Board did not require all the premises which they took over.

The initial livery was orange and white, but was changed to blue and white, rather similar to that which had been used by Lewis & James. In about 1930 the Board adopted what was thought to be a more appropriate livery for a municipal operator, namely maroon with cream bands, black mudguards and lining out in black and gold, and at about the same time the coat of arms began to be displayed on the side of the vehicles: photographs prior to this show a simple belt and buckle device without any arms. This livery was simplified on some vehicles in the mid 1950s to maroon with cream windows, possibly because Leyland simply assumed that that would be the case, and in late 1969 a new livery of light (larkspur) blue and (snowberry) white was adopted.

The original Saurer, registered AX 9617, was ordered by Lewis & James and carried their Western & Sirhowy fleet name, although it never ran in revenue earning service for them. The front steps and door were used by the driver to access the cab area. *(CTC)*

Facing page: Traffic waits at the Pontllanfraith level crossing. At the front of the queue is AX 8060, an AEC 202 of the Blackwood (Mon) Motor Co which was new in July 1925. This company was taken over by Griffin Motor Co later that year and the following year as part of the formation agreement this bus became No.9 in the West Mon fleet. *(CTC)*

Above: Western Valleys commenced replacing its Leyland RAF-type buses with further Leylands, this Leyland SG being new in 1924. Perhaps needless to say, none of these passed to West Mon! *(CTC)*

An example of a Dennis 3-ton chassis with 26-seat bodywork operated by Western Services, a company set up by Griffin and the Watt familiy. These vehicles operated throughout the West Mon area. *(CTC)*

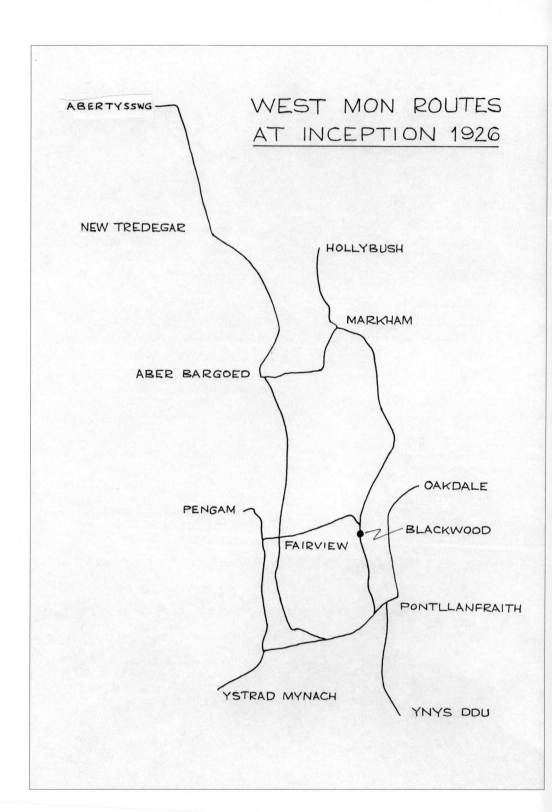

WEST MON ROUTES
AT INCEPTION 1926

ABERTYSSWG

NEW TREDEGAR

HOLLYBUSH

MARKHAM

ABER BARGOED

OAKDALE

PENGAM

BLACKWOOD

FAIRVIEW

PONTLLANFRAITH

YSTRAD MYNACH

YNYS DDU

Chapter Two

EARLY YEARS: 1926-30

The date of completion of the agreements with the companies was 18th October 1926. The first manager of the Board was G Rock, who then left in 1928 to join Lincoln Corporation, which he managed until his retirement in 1951. He was replaced by his assistant, RT Brown, who was to be the most influential figure in the running of the undertaking over the next 30 years. Reginald Theodore Brown (always known as 'RT') was born in the area and had been educated locally at Lewis School, Pengam. He was then employed in the haulage and furniture removal business of Thomas Brown in Blackwood, where he remained until 1922 with a break for service in the First World War. He then moved to manage the Sirhowy Valley bus fleet, remaining with Lewis & James after they took over that operation and then taking on employment with the Board.

The part-time Secretary to the Board was Trevor Griffiths, a Blackwood solicitor, who had served Mynyddislwyn in a similar capacity. His legal expertise was required in years to come as the Board was involved in at least two pieces of heavy litigation. In due course he was replaced by another local solicitor, D Leslie Davies.

In 1927 the Board began to rationalise its running stock and facilities. They negotiated with RT Brown's previous employer, Thomas Brown (who was also a local councillor) to take over his yard in Blackwood High Street temporarily, and in 1931 completed its purchase. It appears that the new area was then incorporated into the garage purchased from Lewis & James in 1926 and previously used by Western & Sirhowy Valleys, and the enlarged premises remained the operating centre throughout the existence of the Board. In 1928 they disposed of the leasehold garage at Ystrad Mynach which they had taken over from Griffin.

The first priority was to extend the Markham-Aberbargoed section of the former Lewis & James service 6 to Bargoed. That extension required the consent of Gellygaer UDC, which had not then begun its own services: the consent was forthcoming, although later relations between the two were sometimes less than friendly.

The proposed extension required vehicles to run up and down Bridge Street, Bargoed, better known

This Leyland, registered B 8692, passed to West Mon from Lewis & James. In this Blackwood High Street view, taken around 1928, it appears that the oriinal body has been replaced with one by Dodson. It is thought that the bus was painted orange and white at this time. *(CTC)*

as Bargoed Hill. This not only involved gradients of 1220ft at 1 in 8, 500ft at 1 in 5 and 250ft at 1 in 4.5, but in addition, and crucially, required drivers to negotiate a very restricted bridge beneath the Brecon & Merthyr Railway branch. This was at the bottom of the hill and immediately beyond the bridge on the hill side was a turn to the right at 90°, followed immediately by another such turn but this time to the left. Extreme care was needed to begin to turn in exactly the right place, especially when descending. In order to avoid the sides of the bridge, the turn could only be made within about 12ins of the optimum point, which was marked: otherwise the nearside of the bus would hit the left hand side of the arch and the offside of the vehicle would hit the right. While this was particularly difficult for the driver coming down the hill, a vehicle travelling up had to tackle the formidable gradient from what was effectively a standing start. The road surface was very poor at the time when the new route was started, with loose gravel on it and some cobblestones which became slippery in wet weather, and it remained unsatisfactory.

Bargoed Hill posed problems which have probably never been equalled in operation in this country and it is a tribute to the driving staff that no serious accident ever took place on it. The route was the preserve of a small number (usually eight) of senior drivers who were paid a special allowance of one old penny an hour in addition to their normal rates.

Lewis & James had wanted to start the service, although they had never got so far as obtaining consent from Gellygaer, which was refused in June 1926, and in any event their progress in this regard was interrupted by the formation of the Board. They were however no doubt aware that in December 1925 South Wales Transport had placed an order for Swiss built Saurer chassis for the steep gradient of the Townhill route in Swansea. SWT began operation of the new vehicles in April 1926 and a fleet of 17 was quickly amassed. In early 1926 Lewis & James approached Saurer and asked for a special vehicle for the Bargoed Hill route fitted with wheel ratchet sprags and with a variable camshaft, so that the engine acted as an additional brake when descending. The vehicle, registered as AX 9617, was delivered in September 1926, between the signing of the agreement to sell the local service and the start of operations by the Board and was tested in Hill Street, Newport, on a steep gradient. It had a B30D body by Dodson to a rather old fashioned design and carried blue livery

The first batch of buses purchased new by West Mon were three Leyland PLSCs (AX 9947/8, WO 72) in 1927, of which one is seen here. Note the absence of crest on the bus at this time. *(CTC)*

MOTOR TRANSPORT

GOODS AND PASSENGER CARRYING BY ROAD.

3ᴰ

No. 1,188. Vol. XLV. COPYRIGHT—REGISTERED AS A NEWSPAPER FOR TRANSMISSION IN THE U.K. DECEMBER 19th, 1927.

15

with Western & Sirhowy Valleys fleetnames. The cost was £1750, which reflected the special order.

Lewis & James never ran the vehicle in service. It was sold on to West Mon in February 1927 for £1500, increasing the Board's debts still further, given fleet number 13, and was initially used by them on other local services. In particular they used it on a new route to Oakdale via the steep Rock & Fountain Hill (Bridge Street and Park Terrace, Blackwood), avoiding the need to run round via Pontllanfraith, and this proved very successful. However, the Saurer was the only vehicle which was capable of using that route and when the Bargoed Hill service began it was abandoned, and thereafter all services to Oakdale ran the longer way round.

The Bargoed Hill route began operation at 3pm on 31st May 1927, originally in the afternoons only. Inspections were required from the Ministry of Transport and the local authority before it

United Counties of Northampton disposed of a batch of Leyland C7 buses after only two years operation. United Counties No. 4, which was later to become West Mon No. 19, (RP 1543), is seen here with what is believed to be a group of the Northampton company's employees. *(CTC)*

was allowed to start, but it soon proved a great success. On 20th June 1927 the manager reported that Western Services were 'running riot' with the Oakdale route since the Saurer had been taken off, and it was at that point resolved to buy a second such vehicle.

The second Saurer (13: WO 974), with a B32R seat body built by United at Lowestoft (the later ECW), was not in fact ordered until 15th August 1927 and arrived in October of the same year. It too was put to work on Bargoed Hill, although the Rock & Fountain service was resurrected for a period in 1928.

The Board's tenuous finances were stretched by the purchase of the two Saurers, but they also required other new and more conventional vehicles to replace some of the unsatisfactory stock which had been taken in. They bought three new Leyland PLSC3 buses with Leyland rear-entrance bodies in 1927 (15-17: AX 9947/8 and WO 72) and at the end of that year acquired five second-hand Leyland C7 vehicles with Dodson bodies from United Counties (1, 11, 19, 21 and 22 RP 1541-5). A sixth was supposed to be included but never appeared, and there is a further mystery in that UCOC records suggest they were sold for £490 each whereas the Board paid £590. They were no

more successful than they had been with United Counties, and lasted only until 1931. It appears that the gearing was incorrect for bus work.

As early as 1927 the idea was floated of a through service to Cardiff, but nothing was done at that stage. Weekly trips were run for pre-booked passengers, some with the Saurer, although these were the subject of complaint from, and the threat of legal action by, Lewis & James, who established a Cardiff service of their own in August 1927 with the consent of Cardiff Corporation. This later passed to Western Welsh.

A long running problem with the Abertysswg route, in which West Mon showed remarkable persistence in attempting to serve a relatively small population which was in any event outside their area, began in late 1927 with the news that heavy traffic was to be banned from the McLaren Bridge, just south of the village: by 1929 a shuttle was in operation on both sides of the bridge, and on 8th March 1930 the road was closed completely for a time. The parallel railway line was also affected by this. The Board did however begin a local service to the new Penllwyn estate in 1928 and to Wyllie at around the same time.

Although on the face of it there was hostility between the Board and the company operators, in fact there were negotiations between them as well. The Board wanted to reach Bargoed rather than terminate at Pengam and resented the presence of the through Newbridge-Deri service of Lewis & James: as early as 1927 it

was proposed that Lewis & James exchange the Blackwood-Bargoed section of that route for the Blackwood-Ynysddu route of West Mon, which was much less frequent than the through service to Newport along the same road. Nothing came of that at that time, but in 1929 the Board used its agreements with the companies to complain of a new arrangement whereby Lewis & James and Western Services agreed to operate jointly between Tredegar, Blackwood and Newport. This led to negotiations and then a reorganisation, in which West Mon acquired the Blackwood-Bargoed section of the Newbridge-Deri route from Lewis & James, and the Bargoed-Deri section was taken over by Gellygaer. Western Services diverted its Blackwood-Pontypool service via Newbridge instead of Oakdale, giving West Mon a monopoly over the Blackwood-Oakdale section. Shortly afterwards, a new road (now the A4048) was build down the valley past Ynysddu, but the Board's service continued every two hours along the old road, with the through service run by the companies using the new route.

In the same year, the Board acquired two more dual-entrance Leylands (2-3: WO 3238/9),

The order for new vehicles in 1929 was placed with Leyland for two LT1s, registered WO 3238/9. These were the frist buses to be delivered in the maroon livery, but again note the absence of a crest on this bus. At this stage Leyland was still building single-decker bodywork with rather plain window frames. *(CTC)*

this time on Lion LT1 chassis, which were later converted to diesel and to rear entrance only, and in that condition served on until 1947, a remarkable record bearing in mind the limited lifespan of most vehicles of that generation. A second-hand ADC was also bought but lasted only a short time as it turned out to be stolen!

By 1929 it was decided that a third hill bus was required. A Thornycroft was demonstrated, but could not cope with the loading requirement, and even Saurer were unable to provide a suitable vehicle on this occasion, although they too carried out a demonstration. The two existing Saurers were also giving cause for concern: the original had collapsed bearings and the newer was showing signs of rot in its bodywork even at that early stage. The inability of other concerns to provide a suitable vehicle left the stage free for Leyland to step in, mindful of the publicity which might result rather than of the profit, if any, from a one-off deal. They provided a Leyland TQ1 Bull goods chassis (1: WO 4625), which was modified with sprag gear to prevent it running backwards, and hand braking on all four wheels. The servo mechanism activated the rear wheel brakes. It was fitted with a Dodson B32D body and was ready for demonstration by September 1930. It passed the test impressively, climbing the hill with a load equivalent to 53 sitting and ten

standing passengers, and entered service on 19th September 1930. Curiously, in October 1930 it was slightly damaged in a runaway accident, not on the hill, but on the steeply graded terminus at Hanbury Square, Bargoed, when the conductor left off the handbrake. The arrival of the Bull allowed the second Saurer to be rebodied and returned to service: the identity of the bodybuilder has not been ascertained.

The fleet was further modernised in 1930 with the acquisition of two new Leyland Tiger TS3s (4-5: WO 4625-6) with Leyland bodies which originally had dual entrances but were later converted to rear entrance. In October 1930 the Board borrowed a blue and white liveried Leyland Lion demonstrator (7: TE 9373) from Leyland, who had constructed it the year before, and then bought it. West Mon bought a number of ex-demonstrators throughout their history, not because they were in the forefront of innovation but rather as they were always anxious to cut

In July 1930 two Leyland TS3s arrived – Nos. 4/5 (WO4245/6), again with Leyland's own bodywork. Of particular interest is the elaborate gold lining out and the fact that a West Mon Board crest now appears on the bus, with the lettering aligned to the foot whereas in all other views it will be seen to be centered. *(CTC)*

down on expenditure and were able in that way to obtain bargains.

The Road Traffic Act 1930, revolutionising the licensing and operation of bus services, was passed on 1st August 1930. A few days before that, on 29th July 1930, there was a conference between representatives of the Board, of Caerphilly UDC, and of Cardiff Corporation. Caerphilly and Cardiff had started a joint service between the two towns in May 1929, which ran along the less direct but easier route through Taff's Well and Nantgarw rather than the shorter but steeply graded road via Thornhill on which the West Mon Saurer had sometimes run while on excursions to Cardiff. Caerphilly also had a route north to Ystrad Mynach, and the Board ran from there to Blackwood, on the service inherited from Griffin, and also from Blackwood to Markham, which was the residue of the Blackwood-Aberbargoed service taken over from Lewis & James, the through service having been split at Markham when the Bargoed Hill route was introduced. The proposal, which was agreed at the conference, was to join up all these services and provide a through service from Cardiff to Markham with an equal number of buses being supplied by each of the three participants and some exchange of staff so that from time to time employees of one organisation drove vehicles belonging to another.

The service began on 1st December 1930, with initially only Caerphilly vehicles running through, but by 1931 there was full participation of all three operators. The route of some 24 miles was far longer than any of the other operations of the Board and required complicated workings with vehicles of Cardiff being accommodated at Blackwood overnight and *vice versa*.

The caption on the original photograph reads 'West Monmouthshire Omnibus Staff 1930'. RT Brown is in the centre of the seated row. The complete absence of female members of staff is noteworthy. *(MYC)*

Leyland was very keen to promote their special order for the Bargoed Hill bus and commissioned a series of pictures graphically illustrating the gradients found on the route. WO 4625, the original Leyland Bull with Dodson two-door body is seen descending the hill. (BCVM/Leyland)

Chapter 3

THE 1930s: DIFFICULT TIMES

In 1931 RT Brown resigned as General Manager of the Board to become an assistant to the South Wales Traffic Commissioners. There were 166 applicants for his post, but the Board made an internal appointment, as it was to do throughout its history. His replacement was FE Goode, who was a councillor in Caerphilly and was thought to have assisted in the establishment of the Cardiff service with that District Council, but he appears not to have been up to the post to which he was elevated and in any event he found that the new responsibilities did not suit him. He managed during his short period in office to antagonise many members of the staff and the situation was very unsatisfactory. In 1933 he resigned voluntarily and reverted to being an inspector, a position he held until his retirement some twenty years later.

Coincidentally, Brown was also less than enchanted with his new post, and he therefore returned to Blackwood to resume his old employment. This time he was to stay for many years, and indeed die in harness. In 1938 he became financial officer in addition to his other responsibilities: previously the accounting work was done by the treasurer of one of the constituent councils. He was highly regarded as an administrator and for his theoretical knowledge, which enabled him to become a Member of the Institute of Transport by submission of a thesis. He was particularly proud of his service as a despatch rider in the First World War, and the other staff were frequently reminded of his experiences in that capacity.

In 1938 the 17 year-old Glyn Harrod Coleman, who was to be the last General Manager of the Board, joined as a junior clerk. He began work as assistant to the secretary, RT Evans, on 1st March 1938, and retired from the Board's successor, Islwyn District Council, on 29th February 1984, never having missed a day through illness. His only time away from the Board during that time was while in the Royal Air Force, 1941-46. Glyn Coleman's unique knowledge of the workings of the Board and his reminiscences of the personalities involved have been of great benefit in compiling this account.

It was somewhat ironic in the light of his career as it turned out that initially Glyn Coleman was not awarded the post, but when the nominated candidate failed the medical he was selected instead. It was his first job after leaving Pontllanfraith Grammar School and was perceived by him as particularly attractive because in the office the staff did not work on Saturday afternoons. In addition, work with a respected local organisation such as the Board offered a desirable alternative to the pit, where five generations of his family had laboured.

At that time the office consisted of about seven people and the Board had about 120 employees in all.

The effect of the Road Traffic Act in the long term was to stabilize the existing route network, but also to inhibit the development of new services. Before that long term effect became apparent there was a certain amount of sorting out to be done. Gellygaer UDC began a service from Bargoed to Blackwood along the same route as the Board, and on 18th May 1931 West Mon lodged formal objection to that. The Traffic Commissioners ordered on 14th October 1931 that the Board run the morning service and the two operators jointly run the afternoon service, so that the Board had a 3:1 proportion of journeys run over the day. The Board also applied to run excursions and tours from Blackwood, but were unsuccessful in that. Other South Wales municipalities made similar applications, all of which were refused. During the lifetime of the West Mon, vehicles were only used for leisure purposes if they were hired by another operator which had the relevant permits.

New vehicles arriving in 1931 were a further Leyland Lion with Leyland body (8: WO 5697) and another ex-demonstrator, although this time one of the first Leyland Cubs built (6: PL 2223) with Leyland 20-seat front-entrance body, built the previous year, and again purchased from Leyland Motors themselves. The third new vehicle in 1931 was another vehicle suitable for use on Bargoed Hill, although since the service at that time ran once in the morning and then hourly (half hourly on Fridays and Saturdays) in the afternoons, the special buses were obviously used elsewhere as well. The second Leyland for the hill was another modified goods chassis, although this time a

A further Leyland TS3 arrived in 1931, No. 8 (WO 5697). As already mentioned the fleet name is now in what has become the standard style, with gold lining out and possibly a cream (or white) roof. By this time Leyland had introduced a more attractive curved window top for its single-deck bodies. *(CTC)*

In 1931 Leyland introduced its KP2 model with Leyland 20-seat body built at its Kingston-on-Thames works where the vast number of vehicles recovered from the First World War vehicle dumps had been rehabilitated. PL 2223 was an early demonstrator and after inspection by the West Mon Board was purchased and became No. 6 in the fleet. It was photographed outside the Leyland factory whilst still on demonstration duties, posed with representatives of the manufacturer. *(CTC)*

more modern TQ3 version of the Bull, again with a Dodson dual-entrance body and special modifications. It is reported that when the Bulls were used on routes other than that up the hill the noise emanating from their overdrive gearboxes led to numerous complaints.

Although the Board by this time had a monopoly of the Blackwood-Oakdale route, they wanted to extend further east to Crumlin, which was in Abercarn UDC. Both Red & White and Ralphs Garages ran on that route, but on 21st January 1932 the former agreed to withdraw in favour of West Mon in return for concessions elsewhere. That still left Ralphs, with whom there were negotiations on the basis that the Board would take over the route but also buy a vehicle from the previous operator at purchase price less 20%. Agreement to that was reached in principle in January 1932 but Ralphs then insisted that it apply to two vehicles rather than one, and in due course this was confirmed. Ralphs gave the route up in about May 1932: it does not appear to have been until over a year later, in June 1933, that the Board put into service two 20-seat Thornycrofts (11/12: WO 2210/2209 respectively) acquired from them: it is difficult to believe that these were not the consideration for the withdrawal.

The service to Ynysddu via the old road had not proved financially viable, and in 1932 Lewis & James agreed not to oppose a move to the new road, particularly since it was then suggested that the Board run only twice a day along a route which was being served very frequently by the companies.

Another new operator did however get into Blackwood in 1932, when Jones Brothers (Commercial Motor Service) of Treharris were granted a licence for their service from Pontypridd via Nelson and Ystrad Mynach: an attempt by them to parallel the Vale of Neath railway line right through to Pontypool proved unsuccessful. They were however to play a part in the development of municipal operation in the Valleys in later years.

Although Gellygaer UDC had not been entirely helpful to the Board, they proposed in 1933 that a wider Joint Transport Board be constituted for the whole area, including Caerphilly, but West Mon were not interested in that or later proposals to the same end.

Once the Crumlin extension had been obtained, the Board's operations settled down to a basic form to which they adhered for many years. Route numbers were applied in the timetables, but never carried on the vehicles, and were in any event changed from time to time.

The Abertysswg route continued to pose problems of its own. The Crumlin route was linked to New Tredegar, producing a run of about 50 minutes with a frequency of between 30 and 60 minutes. This was given the internal number 2. In 1933 it was re-extended to Abertysswg, by which time the service ran via Cefn Fforest rather than the older route via Pontllanfraith: it also connected with the hill bus at Aberbargoed. This route involved strenuous climbing out of Crumlin, where it terminated under the shadow of the lattice viaduct of the Neath-Pontypool railway line high above, and also over Fair View on the other side of Blackwood. There were additional services, numbered 3, which covered parts of the old route and also parts of the indirect service to Ystrad Mynach via Fleur de Lis taken over from Griffin. These afforded connections from New Tredegar to Cardiff by changing at Fair View Corner and Maes-y-Cwmmer, which were carefully arranged in late 1933 when it was learnt that the bridge to Abertysswg was to be reopened. In 1934 the full through service was definitely running, but then the road itself began moving because of a landslide, and the service was again suspended in 1935. The 1937 timetable describes the Abertysswg extension as being 'suspended owing to landslide until further notice'. As the war loomed, there was fresh impetus to reinstate the road all the way through, but for a time from 1939 a shuttle was run from both sides with passengers walking along a footpath over the landslip, which was particularly hazardous in the blackout.

The Blackwood-Bargoed service was given number 4, and Bargoed-Markham was 5. The route to Ynysddu, at this time running to the next settlement, Cwmfelinfach, was known as 6, Wyllie was 7 and Penllwyn 9. The Cardiff-Markham service was sometimes known internally as 1.

In 1934 an experimental service was begun on Friday nights running Bargoed-Aberbargoed-New Tredegar-Phillipstown. This was the first time that the village of Phillipstown had been served, and it was the only service other than that to Markham which had to climb Bargoed Hill.

Although on the surface there was stability in the Board's operations, and despite the economic conditions of the country and of the area, they still wished to expand. There was particular resentment that the Tredegar-Blackwood-Newport service, by then run jointly by Red & White and Western Welsh as successors to the original operators, was more frequent and more profitable than the Board's own routes and ran right through their area. In 1935 they proposed taking over that and the route from Blackwood to Pontypool via Newbridge and Crumlin, but received a hostile response, especially from Western Welsh. The Tredegar-Newport service particularly was regarded at that time as a licence to print money.

It was clear that the right in the 1926 agreements to take over the Lewis & James operations had lapsed once the latter was sold, but the Board wished to exercise the options contained in the Griffin/Valleys/Western Services agreement to take over the services now run by Red & White. On 5th March 1936 the Board had a conference with counsel, as a result of which on 17th April 1936 they served notice on Red & White requiring them

The Board's first bus which was diesel-engined from new arrived in 1935, and no further petrol-engined buses were bought. Number 14, WO 9687, was a Leyland TS6c, the 'c' denoting the fitting of a torque convertor, which was soon replaced with a conventional gear-box. *(BCVM/Leyd)*

to sell their garages and vehicles and also their routes from Tredegar to Newport and Blackwood to Pontypool. The Board may have been short of money, but they did not stint on these proceedings, consulting Gavin Simonds KC and then Fergus Morton KC, both of whom became distinguished Judges, and were among the fashionable leading counsel of their time. Red & White however refused to negotiate, asserting that the Road Traffic Act 1930 had so completely altered the whole scheme of bus services provision that the options were no longer exercisable. Proceedings were begun and indeed the case came before Mr Justice Farwell in the Chancery Division of the High Court in London, by which time the Board were represented by Mr Norman Daynes KC and Red & White by Sir William Jowett, who was later to be Lord Chancellor in the post-war Labour Government. The Judge adjourned the case so that application could be made to the Traffic Commissioners to discover whether, if he found that the Board were correct in law in their claim, a licence would be given to run the services. As a result of that, there was a two day hearing before the Commissioners in September 1938, which was then adjourned to February 1939, when it concluded with a decision in favour of West Mon that if they could establish their legal right to the services the Commissioners saw no objection to

the grant of licences. However the main litigation was not restored before the outbreak of the War.

In other respects, the Board was more circumspect about expansion. In late 1935 a route to Mynyddislwyn village was proposed and rejected because of lack of traffic potential, and the same fate befell another proposal the next year for an extension to the rural hamlet of Manmoel, which lies up a long cul-de-sac east of the Sirhowy. Also in 1936 Bedwas & Machen proposed a through service between Bedwas and Maes-y-Cwmmer, which was of course within their area, via the narrow 'old road' to the east of the Rhymney river, but that did not proceed: nor did a similar proposal by the same authority in 1938 for a Bedwas-Blackwood service via the old road.

The ex-Ralphs Garages Thornycrofts were the only vehicles purchased by the Board between 1931 and 1935, no doubt because of the parlous state of their finances. They did however begin replacing the petrol engines fitted to all their vehicles with oil, as did many other operators at the time, and that of course considerably prolonged the life of the buses concerned. The Saurers were coming to the end of their useful life: 20 (AX 9617) ceased working as a bus in 1934 and was finally withdrawn in 1936, possibly serving as a breakdown tender in the interim. Number 13 (WO 974) ceased bus work in 1939, but definitely served as a tender thereafter, being kept as such until 1946 in order to provide cover in case a vehicle broke down on the hill and required towing. It was fully equipped with a 5-ton crane on the back and was utilised whenever a lorry or van failed on the hill, not least in order to keep the roadway free for the buses.

The minutes of the Board reveal that in 1934 they considered the purchase of a new 'Alpine bus', by which they presumably meant another Leyland, bearing in mind the success of the two in service. An order was placed in the light of the imminent end of at least one of the existing Saurers, and the new 13 (AAX 27) was delivered in August 1935. It was a similar chassis to the earlier two, although this time classified as an Alpine Beaver TSC9 and carried a very handsome Weymann B32R body. The modern appearance of the body contrasted to the antiquated high

set radiator which resembled that on much earlier passenger vehicles. This bus also had an overdrive gearbox, which made it suitable for the fast running required on the southern section of the Cardiff route, on which it was frequently used. Also delivered in 1935 was a Leyland TS6c with Leyland B32R body (14: WO 9687), which later lost its torque convertor in favour of a crash gearbox. It had an early metal framed body, the deficiencies of which caused it to be returned to Leyland for modification later in 1935 and again in 1936. These two vehicles were the first of to be delivered to the Board new with diesel engines, although before then many conversions had been carried out to existing vehicles. The policy of adopting diesel engines was taken up rather earlier than in the case of some other local operators.

In 1937 a further Leyland Tiger was bought, this time on TS8c chassis, and it too was converted to a crash gearbox. It carried Willowbrook B37F bodywork. A more interesting arrival in that year was 11 (BWK 515) a Daimler COG5.40 ex-demonstrator also with Willowbrook body, although this time B39F, making it the largest capacity vehicle in the fleet at that time: it had been on trial at Rhondda Transport. There had been consideration given shortly before this to the purchase of a second-hand double-decker, but the decision was made to buy the Daimler instead and to hope that its increased capacity would alleviate overcrowding at peak periods.

In 1939 a further two Leyland Tigers arrived to TS8c specification, although they were soon fitted with crash gearboxes (12/16: DAX 334/5). They both carried Willowbrook B37F bodies. In that year also an AEC Regal arrived, initially on long term uncharged hire from the manufacturers. This was 19 (KMG 484), which carried a similar Willowbrook body to the Leylands and was the first AEC in the fleet since one taken over from Griffin in 1926.

The outbreak of war thus saw the fleet still entirely single-deck, but still containing a number of vehicles which were elderly by the standards of the time. Apart from the Saurers and the Cub, which was withdrawn in 1939, all the vehicles bought new or as ex-demonstrators by the Board since its inception were still in service in 1939.

A further demonstration vehicle joined the fleet in 1937 following a period with Rhondda Transport. BWK 515 was a Daimler COG5 and introduced the reliable Gardner engine to the fleet. (CTC)

In April 1939 a new Regal, KMG 484, arrived from AEC on extended hire. It was the first new AEC in the fleet but carried a Willowbrook body similar to those fitted to the Leylands and Daimler which had arrived in the previous two years. The single-decker immediately behind the canopy is, of course, from the Red & White fleet of Chepstow, who under an arrangement dating from 1941 were allowed to park a number of vehicles in the West Mon yard. (CTC)

Chapter Four

WAR YEARS and their aftermath

The grim years which followed the outbreak of war imposed enormous strains on public transport all over the country, but perhaps particularly so in areas such as South Wales with heavy industry which had to be kept working. The already extensive special journeys run for the many pits and factories in the area increased, and a notable extension was the provision of miners' buses to North and South Celynen Collieries at Newbridge, which was not otherwise served by the Board. Otherwise there was little change to the routes run, although during the war Cardiff had to concentrate on its local operations and left the Markham service to Caerphilly and West Mon. The Thornycrofts which Cardiff had used on the Markham service became ambulances.

The Board was the subject of lengthy, sympathetic and well-informed articles in Modern Transport for 2nd and 16th November 1940, which were subsequently reprinted as an offprint. In them it was said that labour conditions were so well regarded that only three men had left the Board's employment voluntarily and of those two had subsequently returned.

The road between New Tredegar and Abertysswg was still blocked and despite mention of a temporary road over the landslip in 1943, nothing was done. In late 1944 a strong letter was written asking for a new road to Abertysswg, but still nothing was done and today the whole length of the route which the Board's Tigers took is only a footpath.

The Board was particularly badly affected early on in the War because many of the staff were members of the Territorial Army and were thus called up immediately. The TA was one way in which extra money could be earned and was thus attractive as a means of supplementing income.

The Board's General Manager was appointed as Mechanical Transport Officer for the county for the emergency period. The three Leylands of 1927 vintage and the Leyland Cub were withdrawn in 1940 to become ambulances (15/16) or mobile casualty centres (6/17). The Board's premises were used for the conversion of other vehicles into ambulances and also for the training of female drivers, not of course for the buses but for the new emergency vehicles. In addition to these responsibilities RT Brown was a Major in the Home Guard and he recruited all the staff who had not left for the War into that organisation: the ARP premises were next to the West Mon garage. The guns used by the Home Guard were actually chained up in the office and the ammunition was locked in the safe used for the holding of cash.

As a result of his contribution to the war effort RT Brown was awarded the MBE in 1944.

On the outbreak of hostilities, Glyn Coleman had been left with increased responsibilities because another member of the office staff, Harry Short, was in the TA and had thus been called up early. In 1941 Glyn himself went to join the RAF and did not return until 1946, becoming accounts clerk after the previous occupant of that post married a girl from Hastings and did not return to South Wales. However when Harry Short came back from the services in 1945 he was appointed as an inspector rather than returning to the office and this precipitated the only strike in the history of the Board. The road staff regarded promotion to inspector as their prerogative and objected to his elevation to that position, which led to a week long stoppage in December 1945.

Another former serviceman who returned to employment with the Board was Elvet Williams. He had had an adventurous war, including escaping from a Prisoner of War camp in Germany, a course he decided upon when he received a letter from his fiancée in Blackwood asking to break off their engagement. He later wrote and had published an account of this period entitled Arbeits-Kommando (Gollancz, 1975) which is interesting as it is one of the few such memoirs written not by an officer but by one of the ranks.

The legal proceedings with Red & White continued with no great urgency. A further conference was arranged with counsel as late as January 1943, but shortly afterwards Red & White proposed standing over the action until after the cessation of hostilities. That was agreed and it received no further mention in the minutes thereafter: presumably it was thought that it should just be left to die slowly, and certainly the impetus had gone from it. In order to run the Tredegar-Newport through service satisfactorily the Board would have had to buy a large number of additional vehicles and to expand its infrastructure very considerably.

In 1943 Gellygaer again suggested a Joint Board of themselves, Caerphilly, Bedwas & Machen and West Mon, and again this received little shrift. In 1944 they suggested extending the Blackwood-Bargoed service to Deri as in pre-municipal days, but that again was not taken up.

The Board was in any event fully occupied in running its own operations, which, as in most other industrial areas, were hard pressed. The fleet expansion and the garaging of the many ambulances which had been converted from their own and other local fleets required the purchase in 1943 of additional land from Thomas Brown.

The war brought great pressure to save fuel, and producer gas equipment manufactured by HSG at nearby Treforest was tried out: a petrol engine was also re-installed in one of the vehicles which had been converted to diesel. However by 1941 the need for new vehicles was acute. It appears from contemporary reports that the Board had ordered two further Regals from AEC, and possibly a Leyland in addition, but none of these arrived. The two vehicles which were allocated were both destined for Southern Africa and neither was entirely suitable for the area to which they were sent. Number 6 (EAX 728) was a

Originally destined for Salisbury in Southern Rhodesia (now Zimbabwe), this Weymann-bodied Daimler COG5 is seen at the factory in Surrey before being allocated to West Mon. *(CTC)*

Daimler COG5 with Weymann B35F body which had been ordered for use in Southern Rhodesia (Zimbabwe). Although the Daimler chassis was familiar, the 5-cylinder engine was not ideal for the hilly terrain, and in 1956 it was replaced by a 6-cylinder AEC product. The other new vehicle was the Board's first double-decker, 20 (EAX 729), also a Daimler, but on COG6 chassis, which had been ordered for Johannesburg. Its problem was the highbridge Metro-Cammell H32/26R body, which severely restricted its availability in an area plagued by low railway bridges. Both Daimlers required special dispensation to operate, as they were 8ft wide, and in addition the single-decker was 30ft in length. By the time the British Construction & Use Regulations were amended some years later half-cab single-deckers were becoming outdated and relatively few were built to those dimensions. The remainder of the batch of single-deckers went to Potteries and of the double-deckers to Birmingham Corporation.

From August 1942 to August 1943 the Board was able to hire an ST class AEC Regent with Dodson body (VX 7487, ST 1029) from London Transport, after which the vehicle went on further loan to Rhondda Transport. It was given the fleet number 21 and assisted during a very difficult period. The route through Fleur de Lis on the Blackwood-Bargoed route was altered at this time to avoid a low bridge and thus to permit double-deckers to operate.

Six further double-deckers to Utility standards were then delivered during 1943 and 1944. In 1943

The Board's first double-decker, seen in the upper picture, arrived in 1941 when this Daimler COG6, which had been ordered by Johannesburg, was diverted by the Ministry of War Transport to West Mon. Its highbridge Metro-Cammell body was hardly suitable for operation in the area. *(CTC)*

The next bus to join the fleet, albeit on loan, was an ST-class London Transport AEC Regent, ST 1029, which was used for a year from August 1942. Unfortunately no illustration of it has been found of it with West Mon, and this picture (centre) therefore depicts VX 7487, which had been new in 1930 to Empire, at home in south east London. It was later to pass to Rhondda Transport. *(CTC)*

The first utility double-decker to arrive came in April 1943 and was a Guy Arab I with Strachan body. *(RM)*

The next utility bus to arrive was Daimler CWA6 No. 22, this time with Duple bodywork. By 1956 it had had the upper-deck opening windows replaced but the original single half-drop remained downstairs. *(CTC)*

the Board was allocated 9 (EWO 364) a Guy Arab I with lowbridge Strachan body, 22 (EWO 578) a Daimler CWA6 with lowbridge Duple body, and 21 (EWO 579) another Guy Arab, but this time a Mark II model with highbridge Massey body, which was rebodied to lowbridge configuration by the local firm of Bruce Coachworks in 1950. In 1944 the deliveries were all on Daimler CWA6 chassis with lowbridge bodies, 23 (EWO 858) bodied by Duple and 24 and 25 (EWO 896/5) by Brush. As well as the new vehicles, the two newer hill Leylands were each rebodied by Burlingham in 1943-5 with utility bodies: in neither case was the antiquated radiator style altered. The 1931 Leyland LT3 (8: WO 5697) was also rebodied at this time by Burlingham.

The end of hostilities saw the fleet in urgent need of renewal, while at the same time money continued to be scarce both nationally and locally, and on the other hand the pent-up demand for leisure travel began to be expressed. The Board almost immediately lost its General Manager for six months when Brown was seconded to India to assist with transport problems there, a posting which reflected the high regard in which he was held by those in authority. He was given a carriage of his own in order that he could be moved around the railway network. In his absence Edwin Charles Pugh, who had been employed in the office since the initiation of the Board, was appointed as his Deputy to run matters until his return. The promotion was almost by default, since all the other senior staff were still away in the services, but it stood Pugh in good stead in due course.

In 1945 the business of Jones Brothers (Treharris) Ltd trading as Commercial Bus Service, which had replaced the original partnership, was offered for sale for £35000 to West Mon, the UDCs of Caerphilly, Gellygaer, and Pontypridd, and Merthyr Corporation. Merthyr were uninterested and the other proposed purchasers baulked at the price, which was quickly reduced to £25000. In November of that year they acquired the business, together with routes from Pontypridd to Bedlinog and to Blackwood. The agreement between the four municipalities for operation of these routes was dated 4th February 1946. Each of the purchasers acquired a small number of vehicles: West Mon took 26 (YG 7448) a 1934 Leyland TS6 which had been rebodied in February 1945 with a Burlingham B32F body, and 27 (HB 5948) a Bedford OWB with Duple B32F body which was unique in its new fleet. Neither lasted long with the Board.

It is doubtful whether the purchase of the undertaking was a sensible course for any of the buyers. The routes were not easy to work, and in Caerphilly's case were far distant from their garage. West Mon eliminated the only small private operator in Blackwood, but the service to Pontypridd had limited traffic potential and all but the first two miles or so was outside their area. The purchase had a further unwanted consequence in that proceedings were taken against the Board by a disgruntled local ratepayer, alleging that it had acted outside its powers in using revenue to extend, as opposed to replace, its fleet. The powers so to act were set out in s91 of the Act of 1926 which had set up the Board, but were in fact similar to other powers in other such Acts. The Judge held that the power given to 'maintain' the fleet meant that the Board could both repair and replace existing vehicles from revenue, but there was no power to apply revenue to add to the numbers of the vehicles or indeed to purchase new garages or the like which were required because of an increase in the fleet. The evidence before the Court, given by RT Brown, was that the Board had run about 20 vehicles before the Second World War, but the need for extra works transport had caused an expansion to about 28 by the time of the hearing in late 1946, of which at least two were 'additional' buses and not existing stock kept for longer than normal. The consequence of the decision was that the policy which had been in place since 1938 of buying vehicles from revenue had to be changed so that money was borrowed to finance any expansion: this further constrained the freedom of movement of the management and was not welcomed by the Board or its constituent local authorities. (See Attorney-General v West Monmouthshire Omnibus Board [1947] 1 All ER 248.)

There were a number of variations in the working arrangements for the Jones services, but in general Caerphilly and West Mon ran on the Pontypridd-Nelson-Blackwood service on Mondays to Saturdays, with West Mon running the first bus out of Blackwood and *vice versa*. Pontypridd ran on the service on Sundays and also ran a Pontypridd-Treharris service: Red & White had a separate such service then numbered 81. Gellygaer appear not to have run on the Blackwood service: they already had an established Bargoed-Nelson-Bedlinog service, and they certainly participated in the Pontypridd-Nelson-Bedlinog service which was taken over from Jones and on which Red & White also ran:

this never appeared in West Mon timetables, although Pontypridd-Treharris did. Contemporary Red & White publicity shows every other journey on Pontypridd-Bedlinog as run by themselves and the balance by themselves one week and the 'Joint Councils' the other.

On 19th November 1945 the Board again reached Abertysswg. By this time the attempt to have the direct road cleared had been abandoned, and a new service was begun from New Tredegar via Tirphil and Pontlottyn, requiring much of the route to be run on the western (Glamorganshire) side of the Rhymney valley. It was more of a symbol of the determination not to abandon any territory than an attempt to provide a useful service, and a licence was only obtained after opposition from Gellygaer, Red & White and Hills of Tredegar: with some cooperation with those undertakings more sensible connections could have been developed. In 1946 the service was extended from New Tredegar up to Phillipstown, providing that village with its first regular facilities.

There were fresh calls in the immediate post war period for the commencement of the proposed routes to Manmoel and Mynyddislwyn. The first was the subject of an adverse opinion on the road in 1945, but the following year the consent of Abercarn UDC was obtained, as the road to Manmoel, although not the village itself, was in that authority. The service began in 1947 and was generally one return shopping trip on Friday and one return evening trip on Saturday: initially it was said to be well used, but the traffic potential in the long run was very limited. The Mynyddislwyn service was never approved. Another working which seems to have begun in about 1945 was the running on Sundays only of a few journeys from Blackwood to Markham via Cefn Fforest: these lasted for many years in that form, although in 1945 and for a short time thereafter they were run as through journeys from Bargoed via Markham, Cefn Fforest, and Blackwood to Wyllie.

Cardiff Corporation indicated that it was willing to resume operation on the Markham service, and their participation began again on 31st August 1947, with double-deckers being used for the first time: Cardiff's initial contribution was a Leyland PD1 with Northern Coachbuilders bodywork which was on hire from Hants & Sussex Motor Services Ltd. The joint operators were anxious to extend to Tredegar, which in some ways was

```
W E S T   M O N   O M N I B U S   B O A R D.

TIME-TABLE.   BRYN--COAL HOLE-- FAIR-VIEW.
```

	P.m.	P.m.			A.m.	P.m.	P.m.
BLACKWOOD.	12.45	8.15	Fair-view.		9.32	5.10	9.10
Pontllanfraith.	12.50	8.20	Coal Hole.		9.37	5.15	9.15
Bryn.	12.54	8.24	Bryn.		9.40	5.18	9.18
Coal Hole.	12.57	8.27	Pontllanfraith.		9.44	5.22	9.22
Fair-view.	1.02	8.32	Blackwood.		9.49	5.27	9.27

```
TIME-TABLE.   BLACKWOOD--WYLLIE.
```

					SUNDAY	SERVICE.	
	P.m.	P.m.	P.m.	P.m.	P.m.	P.m.	P.m.
Blackwood.	*12.15	3.15	7.30	9.30	4.20	6.20	8.20
Pontllanfraith.	*12.20	3.20	7.34	9.34	4.25	6.25	8.25
Gelligroes.	*12.25	3.30	7.37	9.37	4.30	6.30	8.30
Wyllie.	*12.30	3.35	7.42	9.42	4.35	6.35	8.35
Wyllie.	*12.30	3.35	7.42	9.42	4.35	6.35	8.35
Gelligroes.	*12.35	3.38	7.47	9.47	4.40	6.40	8.40
Pontllanfraith.	*12.40	3.40	7.50	9.50	4.45	6.45	8.45
Blackwood.	*12.45	3.45	7.54	9.54	4.50	6.50	8.50

```
* Indicates that the service operates only on Fridays.
```

```
TIME-TABLE.   BLACKWOOD--PENLLWYN.
```

	P.m.	P.m.	P.m.
Blackwood.	3.45	7.55	9.55
Pontllanfraith.	3.50	8.00	10.00
Penllwyn.	3.55	8.05	10.05
Penllwyn.	3.55	8.05	10.05
Pontllanfraith.	4.00	8.10	10.10
Blackwood.	4.05	8.15	10.15

This extract from the 1946 timetable gives an interesting snap-shot of some of the restricted services being provided at the time. *(MYC)*

a more logical terminus than Markham, and were encouraged by the Traffic Commissioner, who told Red & White that it would be unreasonable for them to oppose the extension. The through route began operation on 29th February 1948 and at that time was generally hourly on Mondays to Fridays and Sundays and half hourly on Saturdays. There were additional buses between Ystrad Mynach and Markham on Fridays to double the frequency over that section, and on occasion these were somewhat incongruously worked by Cardiff Corporation vehicles. They used the route number 36, whereas neither Caerphilly nor West Mon (which still referred to it internally as 1) displayed such numbers.

The fleet also needed renewal after the war years, as there remained a number of aging single-deckers and in any event the Utility bodies supplied during the war to the new vehicles were generally of poor quality. That position was of course the same all over the country, and there were long waiting lists for vehicles.

In 1947 the Board took delivery of no fewer than five new vehicles. The only double-decker was a Leyland PD1 with Leyland lowbridge bodywork (15: FWO 747). The four single-deckers all had Willowbrook B35F bodies, but two were on Leyland PS1 chassis (5/7: GAX 671/2), and two were on Daimler CVD6 (2/3: GAX 846/7). The latter introduced yet another engine marque to the fleet.

The first post-war single-deck buses, which numbered four in total, arrived in 1947, enabling early LT1 and TS3 Leylands numbered 5, 7, 2 & 3 to be withdrawn. The new vehicles took the numbers of the buses they were replacing, as was the Board's practice, and all had Willowbrook 35-seat bodies. The first two to enter service had Leyland's new post-war single-deck chassis, the model being given the classification PS1. Offside views of these vehicles are not plentiful, hence this slightly cut-off example being included. *(CTC/RMC)*

In the autumn of 1947 the other two single-deckers were put into service and these were Daimler CVD6 models. West Mon already had a number of Daimlers in stock, fitted with either Gardner or AEC engines, but these two introduced the Daimler engine to the fleet. By all accounts this final combination of chassis and body was not highly regarded, being described as 'very slow' by staff. In many fleets wheel chocks would have been used on slopes less severe than this to prevent runaways.*(CTC/RMC)*

The first post-war bus (upper picture) arrived in 1947 and was the only double-decker delivered that year, being a Leyland-bodied Leyland PD1. A characteristic Leyland feature of the time was the painted radiator. *(CTC)*

A fourth double-deck supplier was to be found in the fleet from 1948 when this AEC Regent No. 17 (GWO 422) entered service. Its distinctive Massey body was far removed from the only other body previously received by the undertaking from this builder during the war. It is appropriate that it should be seen (centre picture) at Cardiff bus station as it was only in the year prior to its delivery that the joint operators agreed that this service could be worked by this type of bus. *(CTC)*

The following year another pair of AEC Regents entered service and introduced yet another body-builder to the fleet, the bodies being constructed by Bruce on East Lancs frames. Number 28 (HWO 189) is seen. *(CTC)*

The following year saw three new double-deckers arrive, as the increased loadings in the late 1940s meant that single-deckers were too small for many journeys. Two of the 1948 deliveries were on Leyland PD2/1 chassis with Leyland lowbridge bodies (4/26: GWO522/1) but the third was an AEC Regent with Massey body (17: GWO 422), so the relatively small double-deck fleet then contained vehicles of 4 different manufacturers. All these new deliveries were still 7ft 6ins wide.

In 1949 a further two AEC Regents were received (28/29: HWO189/90), but these had bodywork by Bruce, manufactured locally in Cardiff, although on East Lancs frames. They were contemporary with other such vehicles produced by Bruce for Gellygaer and Green of Haverfordwest. It will be noticed that the numbering system applied to vehicles was somewhat haphazard, with much gap filling. As already mentioned, Bruce rebodied one of the Guy Arabs: the other, 9 (EWO 364) was sent to that company for rebuilding in October 1951 but the coachworks were closing and could not carry out the work, which was instead done by Richards of Newport. Other utilities were rebuilt

in due course as the bodies began to deteriorate.

There was also an urgent need for replacement vehicles for Bargoed Hill. All manufacturers were so hard pressed at the time that there was little enthusiasm for a special order of that nature. However Foden, which was then attempting to break into the passenger market, agreed to supply a PVSC6 chassis, which was duly fitted with sprag brakes on the rear wheels. Ironically in the light of the early history of the Board as set out above, the local Foden agent at that time was JH Lewis, who was one of the original partners of Lewis & James. The bus was registered HWO 590 and took the number of the vehicle it replaced, 1, the Leyland Bull of 1930. The modern appearance of the Foden full-width radiator was somewhat spoiled by the fact that no bodybuilder was available to complete the vehicle within the timescale required, and so the body from the Bull was transferred to the Foden. Since the body dated from 1930, it looked particularly incongruous, although it was partly rebuilt by a local firm, Meredith of Blackwood, before being refitted, in the course of which it lost its front-entrance and became B31R. The amount paid to Meredith however was only £85 0s 2d, so the exercise was not expensive.

Although Foden were prepared to supply a new chassis in 1949 for the Bargoed Hill service, circumstances appertaining at the time meant that no builder was able to provide a body for it. As a result the body on the bus it replaced, a Leyland Bull of 1930, was transferred to the new bus as described in the text. It was later to be rebodied by Willowbrook. *(CTC)*

Chapter Five

THE PROSPEROUS '50s

For the Board, the 1950s were a period of unprecedented prosperity, in which loadings were high and the fleet was gradually converted so that double-deckers formed a majority, a trend which was to be sharply reversed in years to come. 1952 was in fact the peak year for passengers carried.

After the unfortunate strike in 1945, industrial relations settled down and the atmosphere generally was a very happy one. Employment with the Board was then one of the few alternatives locally to coal mining and was therefore highly regarded. One of the motivating factors behind the original establishment of West Mon had been the desire to ensure that transport was kept in local hands. Indeed, so prized was work on the road staff that an unofficial rota was operated, so that each member of the Board would take it in turn to nominate candidates from their particular ward. One of the most influential members of the authority at this time was the repetitively named Councillor Lewis Lewis, whose name was subsequently perpetuated in a road in Blackwood along which the service to Bargoed ran.

Another unusual feature of the Board was that it had early on introduced a scheme for reduced fares for the disabled, blind and elderly, which it was able to do under the terms of its enabling Act. This was a political issue in the early 1950s: a disgruntled ratepayer took proceedings against Birmingham Corporation alleging that it did not have implied powers to put such a scheme into effect and general powers to municipal operators so to act were not granted until a private member's bill was passed in 1955.

The administration remained in the hands of RT Brown, whose standing was recognised when he was elected as President of the Municipal Passenger Transport Association in 1951-2, addressing the conference at Llandudno in September 1952. He was by this time very much a pillar of the community, and sat on the local Magistrates' Bench for some years. In 1954 he was again seconded to advise abroad for a period, in this instance to Aden. His ability was such that he was able to run the Board's affairs without undue difficulty and still give himself time to indulge in a variety of hobbies. At one point after the War he took up the piano accordion and when his wife objected to the constant practising at home he used the office premises to hone his skills, on occasion entertaining the other members of staff. At another time he took up photography seriously and installed a small dark room at the garage, in which one of the traffic officers developed his pictures for him.

The Local Government conditions of employment applied to the Board, which meant that retirement was compulsory at 65 but could be extended for one year by special resolution of the employer. RT Brown found his employment congenial and was anxious not to retire, so his term was extended for the extra year but in June 1959, during that extension, he had a thrombosis and died suddenly at home. He had devoted almost the whole of his adult life to the Board and in many ways shaped it and its spirit. He was replaced by his Deputy, EC Pugh, but his responsibilities were split and Glyn Coleman became financial officer.

The basic route pattern remained the same, although there were some changes. In about 1950 a new local service was begun from Blackwood to the Springfield Estate at Pontllanfraith, and in 1952 another local service commenced around a developing area of Blackwood, to Gordon Road. In the same year an express service from Markham and Blackwood was begun to Ninian Park, Cardiff, for all home games of Cardiff City, who were enjoying a period of great success at that time, and for Welsh internationals. Also at that time, the last remnants of the Blackwood-Pontllanfraith-Fair View service which dated from pre-Board days were withdrawn.

In 1953 the ex-Jones services were reorganised, although the Pontypridd-Blackwood service was not affected. There was further integration with Red & White, and the new pattern allowed for some double-deck operation. The Pontypridd-Nelson-Bedlinog service was run entirely by Red & White (184), and a new Pontypridd-Treharris-Nelson-Bedlinog service (185) was run alternately by Red & White and the joint services. The Pontypridd-Treharris short journeys, also numbered 185, ran only on Saturdays and were run alternate weeks by Red & White and the municipalities.

There were signs that the special problems brought about by Bargoed Hill were beginning

110.-111. The Board Members, Officials and Staff of the West Monmouthshire Omnibus Company, based at Blackwood, in 1951 when they celebrated the 25th anniversary of the foundation of the company. Back row, left to right: W Tippins, D Tucker, K Williams, G Baker, L Evans, G Roper, R Plank, D Bateman, W Smith, L Puzey, W Bram, A Gilbert and J Price. Third row: H Tovey, W John, H Butt, J Smallcombe, C Bartlett, E Powell, E Williams, V Chaytor, R Relleen, W Oakley, I Griffiths, T Haddock, C Williams, and H Jenkins. Second row: C Smith, J Thomas, E Lewis, I Davies, G Tedstone, W Benfield, I Day, C Thomas, G Gibbons, M Watkins, S Jardine, K Tudor, D Edwards and G Gane.Front row: H Short, G Robbins, J Thomas, S Panes, R Jones, J Lane, F Goode, C Pugh, R Brown (Manager), W Alderman (Councillor), E Thomas (Councillor), J Salway (Councillor) and G Adams (Councillor).

Board members and employees gathered together for this official photograph in 1951 to celebrate the Silver Jubilee of the undertaking. Note that the staff now includes women. *(MYC)*

Back row: J Nash, C Garnall, J Steel, E Davies, D George, I Israel, S Lanagan, G Thomas, R Thomas, H Challenger, E Richards and P Parry. Third row: A Salmon, H Powell, H Patience, B Stacey, W Thomas, D Parker, G Adams, L Rolls, D Donovan, R Lewis, W Price, V Thomas and R Cook. Second row: W Lewis, J Mellins, L Jones, B Hancock, V Penaluna, W Noakes, K Gardiner, R Howitt, V Watkins, W O'Neill, D Jones, R Chaffey and S Tillot. Front row: T Griffiths (Solicitor), L Lewis (Councillor), E Butler (Councillor), A Roberts (Councillor), D Williams (Councillor), D Cook (Councillor), G Coleman, B Murrin, O Harris, K White, P Richards, L Walker, E Mitchard, I Thomas, C Walker and E Thomas.

Further Bruce assembled bodies arrived in 1950, but this time on two Daimler CVD6 chassis. The 'DUPLICATE' display on No. 14 (JAX 460), seen here in Caerphilly, seems to have had regular use on the Board's buses. The livery was later to be modified. *(RM)*

For its deliveries in 1953/4 the Board returned to Leyland as its supplier and no doubt it was disappointed when the company ceased body-building the following year. These buses were the first 8ft-wide bodies received (apart from the war-time diversions) and were painted in what might be described as 'Plymouth' style. They were later to receive the standard three cream bands. *(RM)*

to tax the Board, and as early as 1955 they asked for a new road to be constructed in its place. Perhaps the only other sign of retrenchment was that in 1956 the Blackwood-Bargoed service was rediverted under the low bridge at Fleur de Lis, indicating that double-deckers were no longer required on it.

Timetable booklets were issued at intervals throughout the 1950s, as seen alongside. The September 1957 booklet perhaps represented one of the summits of operation in the area. The routes operated at that time, with their general weekday frequency, were as shown on page 45

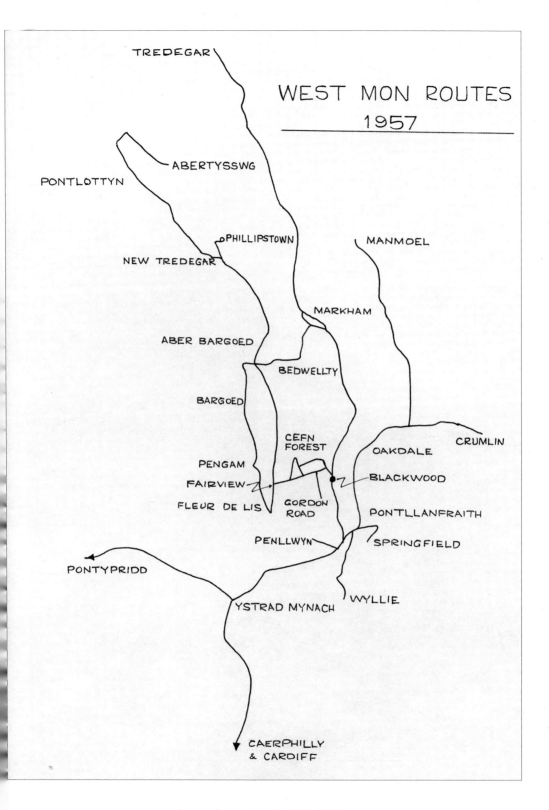

A map of services as in 1957. *(MYC)*

41

This page and opposite: In 1955 the first under-floor engined bus arrived. It was a Leyland PSUC1/1 Tiger Cub with Weymann body. When new it was painted in a revised colour scheme. (STA)

The Tiger Cub's main competitor was the AEC Reliance – two of these arrived in 1956. (CTC)

Prior to this a former AEC Monocoach demonstrator, with Willowbrook body on Park Royal frames had been taken into stock. When new it carried a considerable amount of brightwork. The Monocoach was an attempt by the manufacturer to further reduce weight, and hence improve fuel consumption, by producing an integral-type vehicle. West Mon vehicles could be seen alongside those of Gelligaer (as here), Cardiff and Caerphilly amongst others. *(CTC)*

A new feature in 1957 was the fitment of doors to three new double-deckers. Seen under the erstwhile trolleybus overhead at Cardiff bus station, No. 22 (SAX 187) had Willowbrook bodywork. *(CTC)*

The prototype AEC Mononcoach (NLP 635) which had been new in 1955 was extensively demonstrated to London Transport (its registration number was even in a series utilised for LT service vehicles) prior to West Mon acquiring it in 1957. *(CTC)*

1. Cardiff-Caerphilly-Ystrad Mynach-Pontllanfraith-Blackwood-Markham-Tredegar (hourly, joint with Cardiff and Caerphilly).
2. Crumlin-Oakdale-Pontllanfraith-Blackwood-Fair View-Aberbargoed-New Tredegar (half-hourly).
4. Blackwood-Fair View-Bargoed (half-hourly).
5. Bargoed-Aberbargoed-Markham (hourly).
6. Blackwood-Gordon Road (hourly) or Blackwood-Pontllanfraith- to Springfield (hourly) or Penllwyn (hourly) or Wyllie (about two hourly).
7. Blackwood-Pontllanfraith-Ystrad Mynach-Nelson-Pontypridd (hourly, jointly with Caerphilly).
18. Phillipstown-New Tredegar-Pontlottyn-Abertysswg (hourly).
19. Blackwood-Oakdale-Manmoel (two journeys each way on Fridays & Sats).

In addition there were unnumbered services to Ninian Park and on Sundays the special journeys from Blackwood to Markham, which were treated as part of service 5. Of course there were many works and school workings in addition.

The fleet saw regular replacements arrive during the 1950s. In 1950 two more Daimler CVD6 chassis arrived, although this time double-deckers, again bodied by Bruce in Cardiff: they also rebodied Guy Arab 21 in that year. In 1952 a second Foden for the hill arrived: the Board had asked Bruce to body this also, but by that time they decided to give up bodying buses, and a more expensive contract with Willowbrook was agreed. The resulting vehicle 30 (KWO 368) seated only 31 and appeared at a time when half-cab single-deckers were being superceded nationally. In the following year the other Foden was rebodied in a similar way.

The next few years saw a number of new Leyland double-deckers arrive, although policy towards single-deckers was more mixed, and again reflected the need to save money if at all possible.

In 1953 the deliveries were of two Leylands of model PD2/12 with Leyland lowbridge bodies (8/11: LWO 322/3) and the next year a further such vehicle (12: MWO 389) arrived. All these three buses carried a new simplified livery of maroon with cream windows.

In 1955 the Board began to renew its single-decker fleet. The number of half-cab single-deckers delivered after the war was quite small, unlike neighbouring Gelligaer (as it was spelled after 1953) where vertical-engined single-deckers arrived regularly until 1954. There were two arrivals at the Board in 1955, the first being a

FODENS LIMITED,
ELWORTH WORKS,
SANDBACH.
ENGLAND.

Telephones :
644 SANDBACH (10 lines)
Tel. Address :
FODENWAY, SANDBACH

A M E N D E D

QUOTATION

To Messrs, West Monmouthshire Omnibus Board.

Blackwood.   Mon:

In answer to your Enquiry............17th March 1958,............................we have pleasure in quoting as below :

	PRICES
ONE: Foden fourwheel omnibus chassis ype PVSC/6S, fitted with Gardner 6 cylinder 6LW engine. developing 112 BHP at 1700 RPM, complete with oil bath air filters, 5 speed standard gearbox, 9.00 x 20 front tyres, 900 x 20 outer rears, 8.25 x 20 inner rears, 9.00 x 20 spare wheel complete supplied loose. 32 gallon fuel tank. Heavy duty worm and wheel differential. Axle ratio 5.4 to 1. 24 volt electric lighting and starting equipment with two head and side lamps or other usual accessories. Complete set of loose tools and equipment and generally in accordance with the enclosed leaflet, also ratchet brake fitted to rear wheels.	
ONE: Set of engine bonnets, front grill, scuttle, bulk head plate, front wings, temporary drivers seat.	
The whole of the chassis painted in aluminium rust resisting paint for the sum of..............	£3082. 0. 0
Less 5% discount......................	154 2. 0
	£2927 18. 0

Nett extra, if required.

Air hydraulic brake equipment. - £70. Nett.

Delivery charge to your Depot at Blackwood. Mon.

                    £9. 0. 0. Nett

Delivery :....6/7....weeks from receipt of Order
and/or settlement date of all details.

TERMS OF PAYMENT.
Nett Cash when ready for delivery.

TOTAL PRICE £ 2927. 18. 0

Date........19th May 1958
Our Ref........JHL/OS.
E. & O. E.

For **FODENS LIMITED.** W. H. LEWIS (VEHICLES) LTD.

                                MANAGING DIRECTOR

Foden were keen to retain their links with West Mon and submitted the above quotation
when a replacement for the final pre-war Leyland was required in 1958. *(CTC)*

ROMILLY MOTOR CO. LTD.

SOLE DISTRIBUTORS FOR
SOUTH WALES & MONMOUTHSHIRE

FOR **ACV** VEHICLES

ACCREDITED AGENTS
FOR ALL LEADING
MAKES OF CARS

AUTOMOBILE ENGINEERS
MOTOR BODY BUILDERS

OFFICES AND WORKS
ROMILLY CRESCENT
CARDIFF

TELEGRAMS
ROMOTOR CARDIFF
TELEPHONE
29721/2

OUR REF	YOUR REF	DATE
LP/SH.		18th. June 1958.

R.T.Brown Esq. M.B.E. J.P. A.M. Inst.T.,
West Mon. Omnibus Board,
Blackwood.

Dear Sir,

     Further to our recent conversation concerning a suitable
A.E.C. chassis for operation on your Aberbargoed route. We have
received a recommendation from AEC, and we accordingly enclose our
quotation for the two types of chassis for your consideration.

     The first is the Mercury Mark 1, which is primarily a
12 Ton gross load carrying chassis, but with certain modification
is considered eminently suitable for this particular requirement.
The chassis has a wheelbase of 16'3" is 7'2½" wide, has a 7.75
Litre engine (a vertical model of the Reliance engine) Air Brakes,
Synchromesh gearbox. Axle ratio of 6.28:1 and 9.00 x 20(12 Ply)
front tyres and 9.00 x 20 (10 ply) rear tyres.

     The Second is the Regent Mark V.D3RV Type Chassis. With
a wheelbase of 16'4" is 7'6" wide. 9.6 Litre Engine. Vacuum Brakes,
Synchromesh gearbox, Axle ratio of 6.8:1 9.00 x 20 (12 ply) front
tyres and 9.00 x 20 (10 ply) rear tyres

     We propose if we are successful in obtaining your order,
to fabricate and fit the spragg gear in collaboration with A.E.C.
at our works, after which the chassis could be delivered to your
coachbuilders.

     Assuring you of our best attention at all times.

          We are,
          Yours faithfully,
          For ROMILLY MOTOR CO.LTD.,

          Sales Manager.

AEC were also keen to try to secure the order for the final bus for the Bargoed Hill service,
as will be seen from the above letter. In the event Leyland were successful. *(CTC)*

Leyland Tiger Cub with Weymann B44F body (18: MWO 709), which showed the advantage of the underfloor engine so far as seating capacity is concerned. The second was perhaps more interesting, being another ex-demonstrator (16: 168 DMU), a rare AEC Monocoach with Willowbrook B45F body bought from the manufacturers but new earlier that year.

The next year saw two further AEC single-deckers appear on the scene, but 10 and 19 (PWO 479/80) were more conventional Reliances with Willowbrook B43F bodies.

In 1957 three new double-deckers arrived, again on the trusted Leyland PD2 chassis, but this time of variant PD2/40. They bore Willowbrook bodies and were fitted with platform doors, another new feature: (9/22/25: SAX 186-8). In that year however another ex-demonstrator bargain arrived in the form of AEC Monocoach/Park Royal B45F 20 (NLP 635), which had been manufactured in 1953 and thus predated its colleague. It was a

The final bus for the Bargoed Hill service arrived in 1959 and the Willowbrook body was fitted to a modified double-deck Leyland PD2/38 chassis. *(CTC)*

well-known vehicle as it was not only a prototype but also had run for London Transport in Green Line livery.

In 1958 only one new vehicle was delivered, 23 (TAX 710), which was a further Leyland/Willowbrook double-decker with platform doors. The next year, 1959, saw one of the Board's most interesting vehicles appear. It had become clear that three vehicles capable of working the hill were required and the last of the Leylands was reaching the end of its life. An enquiry was made of Foden amongst others for a replacement, but their quotation was considerably more than those tendered by AEC and Leyland. The latter was chosen, and the new vehicle arrived in March 1959. It was based on a modified PD2/38 double-decker chassis, and was only 7ft 6ins wide, by then an unusual specification: the rear extension was cut off and the customary sprag brakes were fitted. Willowbrook built a 31-seat half-cab body of a style which harked back about ten years: very few half-cab bodies were made after this date, although a number of special low-heght vehicles on AEC double-decker chassis were supplied to South Wales Transport for service in the Llanelli docks.

Chapter Six

THE SIXTIES:

Economic problems surface

It is difficult to resist the conclusion that the Board had become set in its ways by the 1960s. It continued to take delivery of exposed radiator Leyland double-deckers which were undoubtedly robust, but were becoming old fashioned. More importantly, there was no one-man operation, and labour relations on this and other issues deteriorated sharply throughout the decade.

The General Manager, EC Pugh, was not as able as his predecessor and was unpopular with some staff. He tended to shut himself in his office and on occasion to display sudden and unpredictable explosions of temper, which made working with him difficult. He failed to take promote any new initiatives to take account of the changing circumstances.

There was then a serious and damaging dispute in 1968, which led to a ban on overtime and standing passengers, and led to the Board having as a matter of necessity rather than choice to buy second-hand rather than new vehicles. All was however not negative, and at the end of the decade a new office was built and an extension constructed for the depot: an artistic-minded employee arranged for the words 'West Mon Omnibus Board' to be set out in white pebbles to sign the site. A further part of the area was sold off for a filling station.

In 1968 Glyn Coleman was promoted to Deputy General Manager: he was undoubtedly frustrated by not having reached the top position by that time. Apart from war service, he had already served 30 years with the Board, and in his application he said with some justification that it was 'quite different from the normal municipal undertaking', in arguing why an internal candidate should be appointed. In 1953 he had enrolled as a student with the Institute of Transport, becoming an Associate Member in 1957, and in 1973 he was made a Fellow.

In 1968 Caerphilly again proposed a joint board of the local municipalities, and it was again rejected. However the concord which had led to joint operation on the ex-Jones services was

The second Leyland Tiger Cub to arrive was No. 6 (XWO 3420) in 1960. This time Willowbrook provided the BET-style body, which was noteworthy for the large destination indicator, part of which was initially blanked off. The Tiger Cub was to be supplied as the standard single-decker until 1968. By now, single-deck West Mon vehicles in Cardiff were unusual. *(CTC)*

The only Longwell Green body delivered to the Board was on this Leyland PD2/40 in 1960. Around the same time both neighbouring Gelligaer UDC and Bedwas & Machen UDC took similar bodies. Note the narrow cream band above lower deck windows. *(CTC)*

A year later the Board went back to Massey for its choice of double-deck bodies, and was to remain with this builder until the final double-decker was delivered. Number 21 (260 BAX) was provided with a long handle to operate the destination screen. *(RM)*

beginning to fall apart. Caerphilly gave notice of their intention to withdraw in June 1968 and Pontypridd in August of that year. It is rather surprising that when in 1970 Western Welsh enquired about taking the Pontypridd-Blackwood service over, they were not welcomed with open arms, but in fact West Mon showed their customary unwillingness to relinquish territory, and even thought of expansion: even in 1969 the question of a through New Tredegar-Blackwood-Newport service was raised but not taken further.

In 1963 the Manmoel service, which had long since ceased to be economic, was handed over to local operator Glyn Evans, who ran it with a minibus. During this period the Abertysswg service was reduced to two hourly beyond Tirphil, and the spare capacity so released was used for two short local services from New Tredegar to Greenfield and to Jubilee Terrace.

The most substantial change to the Board's operations in this decade was however the decision to by-pass Bargoed Hill, which took effect in December 1963. Unfortunately the only volume of the West Mon Board records which appears to have gone missing is that for 1959-1968, but a full minute looking back at the decision was filed on 11th November 1970 and an interesting article on the route appeared in the Leyland Journal for January-February 1964. It is usually said that the reason for the change was to serve new housing, but that is an oversimplification. The Board had been asking for some years for the railway bridge to be removed, as it was that which made operation on the hill so difficult: vehicles could not gather any speed before attempting the ascent because of the need to go so slowly under the arch and then turn. The minute indicates that there were two main reasons for the change: the first was the restriction caused by having to keep in stock three low capacity buses which were of little use elsewhere on the system, and the second was that the growth of new housing, especially at Aberbargoed, which was on the existing route, meant that the vehicles were often crowded. The three hill buses were reported in 1963 as only running about 15000 miles per annum each, whereas the average for the other vehicles in the fleet was about 32000. Further, because so much of their running was done in bottom gear, they required far more frequent servicing and tyre changes than did the rest of the fleet.

The result of the change was to lengthen the route very considerably, although the extra expense was more than compensated for by the ability to dispense with the special vehicles and by the extra capacity of their replacements. In order to get from Aberbargoed down to Bargoed, buses had to travel south along the eastern side of the river, cross the river at Pengam, and then go back north along the western side. This was a route which was already used when bad weather made the hill impassable, but whereas then the service was run on a limited stop basis the new arrangement did serve new housing which had been built between Fair View and Aberbargoed. After about six months the route taken through the existing estate at Aberbargoed was shortened to speed up journeys, but the problem was compounded in early 1968 when a one-way system caused by difficulties at Pengam diverted all vehicles travelling towards Bargoed via Fair View corner, even further off route, and then in 1969 the railway bridge at Pengam was closed, leading to services in both direction having to go

An unusual vehicle to be found in any fleet was this 1962 11-seat Commer minibus. It was barely long enough to accommodate the Board's fleet name. *(CTC)*

round that diversion. The reaction to the extension of running time so caused was to make the section to Bedwellty village a loop served only in one direction. A passenger to Bedwellty therefore had to travel via Markham, where there was in any event a loop from the village ('Markham Top') down to the main road, where the service terminated.

The first vehicle in 1960 was interesting. Although 24 (XWO 473) was another Leyland PD2/40, it carried bodywork by Longwell Green of Bristol, a small builder with a following among other South Wales municipalities but which had never supplied the Board: indeed this was to remain a unique example, although they did supply the body for West Mon's AEC matador towing vehicle. The new decade then saw the arrival of further Leyland Tiger Cubs, 6 (XWO 342) with Willowbrook B45F body in 1960 and 2/3 (125-6 BAX) with Weymann bodies of similar configuration the following year. The latter vehicles had a somewhat unusual appearance for their date as they had metal mouldings on the side similar to those which had been used on the integral Olympic design, and which resembled contemporary vehicles for Edinburgh Corporation. A further Leyland PD2/40 with Massey body was delivered in the same year (21: 260 BAX) and two more in 1962 (14/27: 203/4 CWO). Another

In 1966 the chassis of the seven year-old Leyland PD2/38, purchased for the Bargoed Hill service, was rebuilt by West Mon and fitted with a new Massey body as shown. *(CTC)*

Facing page top: The last double-deck body ordered by the Board arrived in 1966 on No. 28 (KWO 134D), by which time the lowbridge Massey body was looking distinctly dated. *(CTC)*

unusual vehicle for a public authority arrived that year in the form of an 11-seat Commer minibus (19: 296 FAX) which was used mainly for personnel movement.

The 1963 and 1964 deliveries were each for two Leyland Tiger Cubs with Willowbrook bodies, 5/7 (404/5 HAX) in 1963 and 1/30 (AWO 528/32B) in 1964. They took the numbers of the two Fodens, which were then withdrawn, having been used on general duties after the cessation of the hill route.

In 1965 two further double-deckers arrived in the form of 15 and 17 (EWO 195C and GWO 351C) which again were on traditional exposed radiator Leyland PD2/40 chassis with equally traditional lowbridge bodies by Massey. Another arrived the following year (28: KWO 134D), and in addition the former Bargoed Hill Leyland PD2/38 was rebodied as a double-decker by Massey in July 1966. These were very late

Above: Force of circumstances led to the purchase in 1967 of two former Western Welsh Tiger Cubs, the second of which, No. 20 (JBO 118), is seen ironically in Cardiff, where the company's Head Office was situated, although the actual bus in question had been based at Cwmbran depot. *(RM)*

Right: The first Leyland Leopard, No. 29 (OAX 160F), arrived the following year and was fitted with a BET-style Willowbrook body which was not dissimilar from that fitted eight years previously to the Tiger Cub seen on page 45. *(CTC)*

The distinctive Saunders-Roe body was to be found on the final Tiger Cub acquired by West Mon in 1968, No. 10 (FCH 19) which had been new to East Midlands Motor Services in 1954. (RM)

Top: Also new to East Midlands, but obtained from a dealer, were two 1956 Leyland PD2/20s with Metro-Cammell bodies incorporating concealed radiators, sometimes referred to as 'new look' fronts. The dealer perhaps failed to mention that whilst one had vacuum brakes, the other had air. A driver's nightmare! *(CTC)*

Above: The only new vehicle to arrive in 1969 was this BMC 250 which replaced the Commer seen on page 47. Number 19 (UAX 222H) was the first in blue and white livery and retained its fleet number for only one year. Sharp eyes will note the out-of-area registration plate on the car – VFY 1 belongs to the former Southport Traffic Superintendent, later General Manager at neighbouring Gelligaer, who recorded this scene. *(RM)*

examples of the lowbridge configuration, which was unpopular with passengers because of the 4 abreast upstairs seating, but was required in the area: the only highbridge double-deckers used were taken into stock in the emergency conditions of the Second World War and were very restricted in operation because of the extra height. The very last lowbridge double-decker built was delivered to Bedwas & Machen in 1968 on a Leyland PD3/4 chassis.

There is no doubt however that 1966 marked the end of an era for the Board. Number 28 was the last new double-decker delivered, and the pressure to adopt one-man operation gathered pace after the bitter industrial dispute of 1968. In

1967 the Board bought two 13 year-old Leyland Tiger Cubs with Weymann bodies from Western Welsh: initially they too were used as two-man vehicles (16/20: JBO 117/8). The following year they were able to afford just one new bus, the first Leyland Leopard in the fleet, which carried Willowbrook B45F bodywork (29: OAX 160F), but they also bought another second-hand Tiger Cub, this time from RI Davies of Tredegar, although it had been new to Trent in 1954 (10: FCH 19). It carried Saunders Roe bodywork. They also bought two ex-East Midland Metro Cammell bodied Leyland Titans (11/12: UNN 111/5) from a dealer. These introduced 'tin fronts' to the fleet, and indeed were unique in that respect among major operators in the area, but like the other second-hand acquisitions were short term expedients. None of these vehicles lasted very long with the Board.

In November 1969 No. 13 became the first double-decker to be repainted into the blue and white livery. The application of the new scheme was in fact to be non-standard, a greater area of white being found on this bus. A new style of fleet name also appeared. (CTC)

An unexpectedly significant vehicle was the only delivery in 1969. This was 19 (UAX 222H) a BMC 12-seat minibus which was a replacement for the Commer. For some reason the manufacturers were unable to deliver the vehicle in the Board's livery, and it arrived in light blue and white. The members inspected it, and on 2nd October 1969 resolved to adopt the colours so used for the entire fleet. This decision was also precipitated by a change in attitude by the previous paint suppliers, Brown Brothers. Supplies of maroon of the particular shade required (which was unique to the Board) were kept by them at their Cardiff depot and West Mon were not required to pay for the paint until it was actually required: they were therefore able to have their vehicles touched up or even completely refurbished at short notice without the need to maintain expensive stock. At this time it was indicated that this practice was uneconomic and could no longer continue.

As with many decisions intended to modernise an image, the effect was not universally appreciated and certainly something was lost. At the same time the traditional 'WEST MON' with the Board's arms between the words was abandoned and 'West Mon Omnibus Board' applied in script.

Chapter 7
THE SEVENTIES

The Board was not alone among transport operators in facing serious problems at the end of the 1960s, but it was not well placed to deal with them. A further outbreak of industrial unrest in 1970 weakened its position still further, and it was clear that drastic action was required to remedy the situation.

EC Pugh was in fact expected to retire as General Manager in 1971 and Glyn Coleman was naturally very anxious to succeed him. However Pugh wanted to stay on, and was somewhat vague about the exact date of his birth. He stayed until 1972, when he applied for the one year extension which had been granted to his predecessor, the true position finally became clear and he left: Glyn Coleman was then finally appointed to the position, which he combined with that of Chief Financial Officer, as had RT Brown.

There were only minor developments to the routes during the 1970-4 period: for example in 1972 the Gordon Road service was altered to serve new housing and also extended to form a circular. The Springfield service was also given a long terminal loop through the estate, which eliminated a dangerous exit on to the main road. In the same year the works were finally completed to enable the Bargoed-Markham service to resume its designated route at Pengam.

What turned out to be the last years of the Board brought a substantial influx of new single-deck vehicles. In 1970 three new Leopards arrived, all with Willowbrook B47F bodies, in the new livery: 4/12/19 (VAX 62-4H). As with the 1968 vehicle, these were all of the shorter PSU4 variant, which was much less common than the longer PSU3. The following three years however saw the arrival of twelve further new Leopards, transforming the fleet. In 1971 8, 10 and 26 (YAX993-5J) arrived, all of the 36ft long PSU3 type, with Willowbrook B53F bodies which held as many as the double-deckers they were replacing. Further, these three were equipped for one-man operation from the beginning. The following year two batches were delivered, both on PSU3 chassis with Willowbrook bodies: the first, consisting of 11, 16, and 24 (CAX 764-6K) were B47F configuration and the second, 9, 18 and 20 (GAX 568-70L) had B53F bodies. The following year another three shorter vehicles arrived, 6, 22 and 25 (OAX 972-4M). The 15 vehicles delivered in 1970-3 were a determined effort to modernise the fleet, which had fallen far behind most others in the country. The last three Leopards were however to be the last vehicles delivered to the Board.

As part of the belated modernisation drive, the Bell Punch tickets then in use, which had replaced the original Willebrew system, were replaced in 1971 by Almex products which were far more suitable for one-man operation.

The end of the Board came somewhat unexpectedly, and was the result of the widespread changes in administration brought about by the Local Government Act 1972, which took effect from 1st April 1974. A new county of Mid-

The 1970's saw a determined attempt by the Board to modernise its image and fleet, as has been seen by the change of livery. Thus no less than 15 Leyland Leopards with more modern Willowbrook bodies entered service between 1970 and 1973, being a mixture of 33ft and 36ft long buses. Number 12 (VAX 63H) was one of the initial trio of the shorter length. *(CTC)*

Glamorgan was created, and to it were transferred by Schedule 4 three areas which had previously been part of Monmouthshire, namely the Urban Districts of Rhymney and of Bedwas & Machen, and also the Aberbargoed, Cwmsfyiog, New Tredegar and Phillipstown wards of the former Bedwellty UD (wards which included Bedwellty Village itself). The remainder of Bedwellty UD and the whole of Mynyddislwyn UD were incorporated into the new Islwyn District, which included also the former Risca and Abercarn UDs, and was in the renamed County of Gwent. The transferred areas, together with Caerphilly, Bedwas & Machen and Rhymney UDs and most of Gelligaer UD, formed the new Rhymney Valley District.

The future of Joint Boards was specifically provided for in section 263 of the Act. The position was that, by virtue of section 263(2), where a new authority took over the whole of the area in which such a board operated, then all the assets of the board passed to the new authority and the board itself was dissolved. This did not apply to the West Monmouthshire Omnibus Board, because the 4 wards mentioned were not to be part of Islwyn. The Board's position was governed by s263(1), which provided that where all the area in which a board operated was not transferred to one new authority, then the board continued in operation with the substitution of the new authorities for the old. On the face of it therefore West Mon would continue as a joint board of Islwyn and Rhymney Valley Districts, with the latter as junior partner.

For a long time, it was assumed that that is what would happen, but there was a certain amount of vacillation. The shadow administration of the new Rhymney Valley District Council, which of course had its own undertaking to run, first did not, then did, want to participate. By the time they decided they did want to take part, the Islwyn side decided that they wanted to run their own transport without interference from any other authority, and thus the Board's fate was sealed. As it had been established under statute, it could only be dissolved in the same way, but a power to dissolve joint boards and other such organisations was reserved to the Minister under section 254 of the Act.

In order to give effect to the changes to joint undertakings and the like required by the new legislation, the Minister produced a statutory instrument in 1973. Because of the uncertainty over West Mon, it was not included in that principal instrument, and was included in a sweeping up ancillary instrument with the convoluted title of the Local Authorities etc. Wales (Property etc.: Further Provision) Order 1974: this was signed only on 14th March 1974, which demonstrates the last minute nature of what was done. Paragraph 4(16) of the order transferred the assets of the Board to Islwyn Borough Council.

The last meeting of the Board was on 27th March 1974 and on 1st April 1974 it ceased to exist.

The final batch of buses delivered to the Board included this Leyland Leopard No. 6 (OAX 972M), seen at Blackwood. (RM)

Chapter 8

POSTSCRIPT

The outside observer who looked at the position of the smaller Welsh municipal operators in 1974 would no doubt be surprised that 30 years later only Islwyn still survives. That fact is made the more extraordinary by the fact that in the next round of Welsh Local Government reorganisation, in 1995, Islwyn was incorporated into a new Caerphilly Borough, which had lost its earlier undertaking in the aftermath of deregulation, as had Cynon Valley (Aberdare), Merthyr, and Taff-Ely (Pontypridd).

It is not the purpose of this work to deal with the history of Islwyn DC's operations after the demise of the Board, but, in summary, the double-deckers disappeared, the fleet became in due course wholly one-man operated, and midibuses were acquired for new services. The Abertysswg route, which after the changes in 1974 lay wholly outside Islwyn, was handed over to Rhymney Valley in exchange for full operation of the Blackwood-Bargoed service. Bargoed Hill was very much altered by the removal of the railway bridge and the widening of the road: indeed, on 9th January 1989 buses returned to the hill on a Bargoed-Markham service, although with modern vehicles, and particularly with the removal of the sharp turns under the bridge, it presented much less of a challenge than it had previously. The Board's old garage was handed over for redevelopment and IDC relocated to new premises in Pontllanfraith. Glyn Coleman continued to run the undertaking under the auspices of Islwyn but with the new title of Transport Manager until his retirement in 1984, and his responsibilities were extended to cover all the vehicles operated by the new local authority, even down to grass cutting machines. Previously the Board had only maintained such ancillary vehicles for Bedwellty but had no operational responsibility for them.

The West Monmouthshire Omnibus Board had an interest and evocation far beyond its size and it is hoped that this short account brings back memories in those who knew it and arouses the interest of those who did not.

Members of the last West Monmouthshire Omnibus Board record their place in history. *(MYC)*

127. The last regular board meeting of the West Monmouthshire Omnibus Board was held on 4th March 1974. From its birth in 1926 the company had been operated jointly by the councils of Bedwellty and Mynyddislwyn. Standing: B. Mantle (Bedwellty), G.C. Garrett (Bedwellty), E.J. Butler (Bedwellty), T.J. Duckham (Mynyddislwyn). Seated G.H. Coleman FCIT (General Manager and Chief Financial Officer), J.D. Turner (Bedwellty) Vice Chairman, A.G. Mayo (Mynyddislwyn) Chairman, Mrs M.R. Powell (Bedwellty), D. Leslie Davies Solicitor (Clerk to the board). Absent: H. Lewis (Bedwellty), C.C. Thomas (Mynyddislwyn).

Appendix 1
'THE HILL'

Many transport students and enthusiasts, if asked about the West Mon fleet, would almost certainly make reference to the Bargoed Hill service, even if they knew little else about the undertaking. Over the years both the professional trade press and enthusiasts' magazines devoted many pages on articles about this unique service. From Saurers' adverts in 1928 to accounts dealing with the by-passing of the hill in 1963 much was written about the route. For its length and the number of buses involved it was pro-rata probably photographed during its time as much as any other service in the country.

The next few pages are therefore devoted to this remarkable facility and recall an age that has long since disappeared.

The panoramic view, taken by Leyland for an article in the Leyland Journal for July 1935, appears to include at least one of the Saurers. It shows a 'step-by-step' view of the various lengths of the differing gradients on the route. (MYC)

This diagram of the route, also produced by Leyland, identifies the line taken up the hill, with the black circle marking the location of the gas-holder at the bottom and the sharp turns under the railway bridge. (CTC)

Here the original Leyland completes the 'zig-zag' under the railway before tackling the steepest part of the climb. (STA)

In what were obviously two posed views, WO 4625 stands outside the local hostelry. Although facing down the hill in the upper picture, it almost certainly was not going to Markham. In comparing the pictures on this page with the panoramic hill view, it would appear that there was some doubt as to whether this public house was intended for one or several 'Travellers'. The body on this Leyland TQ1 was by Christopher Dodson of Willesden, north London, and a firm which succumbed to market pressure before the Second World War. The body, however, was transferred to the first Foden in 1948 as shown on page 67. *(CTC)*

The 1931 Leyland Bull (WO 5913) approaches the top of the gradient in this postwar view. Its original Leyland body had been replaced with this new Burlingham one in 1946. In the background is the (then) Glamorgan side of the valley (RM)

The final pre-war 'hill' bus arrived in 1935 as seen opposite. It was a Leyland Alpine Beaver (AAX 27) and is operating in the reverse direction from the upper picture. In this war-time view the gradient experienced on the service is again dramatically demonstrated. The cloud being emitted by the side of the bus could merely be dust, as parts of the hill were poorly surfaced, with macadam on one side and loose gravel on the other, or it could be exhaust, as the low gearing of the special buses used on the service meant that they literally had to be driven down hill. (CTC)

The gradient diagram below accompanied an article published by Leyland in 1964. (CTC)

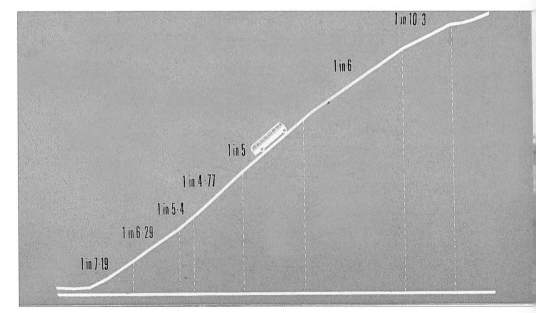

Two more views of the hazard presented by the railway bridges, again illustrated with, in the upper view, another war-time picture of AAX 27. The same bus clearly demonstrates in the lower view the requirement to obtain a full right-hand lock once the bridge had been negotiated when traveling uphill. *(CTC both)*

Seen here (in the upper picture) at the Bargoed terminus of the route complete with dog, boy and bicycle, but seemingly few passengers, Foden No. 1 (HWO 590) still has its original (second-hand) Dodson body, albeit converted to rear entrance only. In the lower view it is about to descend the hill. By this time it had received its replacement Willowbrook body. The less than perfect road surface will again be noted. *(RM both)*

Further down the hill HWO 590, in original condition, produces another cloud as it traverses the challenging road surface. Clearly the highways department had their reasons for wanting the differing surfaces for up and down hill. To the authors' knowledge there were no runaways throughout the duration of the service, probably due to the fact that only specially trained drivers on these bespoke vehicles were involved. *(CTC)*

The final Foden materialised as KWO 368 in 1952, this time with a Willowbrook 31-seat body from new. *(RM)*

The final hill bus arrived in 1959 as seen above and overleaf. Plans were already under consideration to by-pass the hill and the chassis supplier reverted to Leyland, who therefore supplied a double-deck PD2/38 chassis, specially modified to take the now hill-standard 31-seat Willowbrook body, but capable of taking a conventional double-deck body at some point in the future. *(CTC both)*

The roof of the gas-holder, marking the bottom of the valley, together with the hill-side on the opposite side, form a backdrop in this study of the hill route. The final hill bus, No.11 (UWO 688) makes the steady climb on its way to Markham. *(CTC)*

Below the 1957 time table shows why a maximum of three buses only (which nevertheless represented around 10% of the fleet strength) was required on a service that at best ran every 30 minutes. *(MYC)*

ROUTE No. 5
MARKHAM—BARGOED

	WEEKDAYS				FRIDAYS AND SATURDAYS (Additional Service)				SUNDAYS				
	am	am	am		p m	pm	pm		pm	pm	pm		pm
MARKHAM	8 35	10 5	11 5		10 5	2 35	3 35		8 35	3 5	4 5		9 5
Markham top	8 40	10 10	11 10		10 10	2 40	3 40	And every hour until	8 40	3 10	4 15	And every hour until	9 10
Bedwellty	8 43	10 13	11 13	And every hour until	10 13	2 43	3 43		8 43	3 20	4 20		9 20
Aberbargoed (arrive)	8 50	10 20	11 20		10 20	2 50	3 50		8 50	3 25	4 25		9 25
Aberbargoed (depart)	8 50	10 25	11 25		10 25	2 55	3 55		8 55	3 35	4 35		9 35
BARGOED	9 0	10 35	11 35		10 35	3 5	4 5		9 5				

	am	am	am		p m	pm	pm		pm	pm	pm		pm
BARGOED	9 10	10 40	11 40		10 40	3 10	4 10		9 10	3 40	4 40		9 40
Aberbargoed (depart)	9 20	10 50	11 50		10 50	3 20	4 20	And every hour until	9 20	3 50	4 50	And every hour until	9 50
Bedwellty	9 28	10 58	11 58	And every hour until	10 58	3 28	4 28			3 58	4 58		9 58
Markham top	9 32	11 2	12 2		11 2	3 32	4 32			4 2	5 2		10 2
MARKHAM	9 35	11 5	12 5		11 5	3 35	4 35			4 5	5 5		10 5

NOTE—The bus leaving Bargoed at 9.10 p.m. on Fridays and Saturdays only will return to Bargoed and duplicate the bus leaving Bargoed at 9.40 p.m. for Markham.

Appendix 2
DETAILED FLEETLIST

NOTE

The tables below show the fleet number, registration number, chassis, chassis number, bodybuilder, layout (using standard abbreviations) and date new of all vehicles. Additional notes are below the tables. The vehicles acquired after the commencement of operations are listed by year with new vehicles followed by acquired, each in chronological order.

VEHICLES ACQUIRED FROM LEWIS & JAMES LTD, 1926

1	AX6867	Leyland 36/40hp			B30	11/24
2	B8692	Leyland 36/40hp			B30	/20
3	AX1697	Leyland RAF			B30	5/20
4	AX5484	Leyland RAF	5263	Dodson	B30	9/23
5	L6431	Daimler CK	3614		B26	2/20
6	NY3965	Thornycroft BT	10092	J Norman?	B26	9/23
7	AX7390	Thornycroft A1	11304	J Norman?	B20	4/25

GENERAL NOTES

(1)   The seating capacities set out are the official versions which do not always agree with the licensed seating: 5 was licensed as a 25-seater until 09/28 when it became a 20-seater; 6 was originally a 24-seater that became 25.

(2)   One of the Leylands had a body by Bristol.

(3)   1-3 and 5-7 were all ex Sirhowy Valley Motor Transport and passed to Lewis & James in 10/25. They were believed to be numbered 28-34 but one of those numbers was for another Thornycroft.

(4)   One of the Leylands had an accident at Ynysddu in the early years of the Board and was dismantled.

PARTICULAR NOTES BY VEHICLE NUMBER

1   Withdrawn 10/26, disposal uncertain.

2   Rebodied by Dodson B30 and rebuilt between 10/25 and 10/26. It was withdrawn in 12/29 and possibly disposed of to Leyland in part exchange.

3   Registered to Phillpotts Brothers, Newbridge as an AEC 40 hp charabanc. It was withdrawn in 12/29 and possibly disposed of to Leyland in part exchange.

4   New to Western Valleys as number 12. Chassis was new in 1916. It was probably withdrawn in 12/29 and possibly disposed of to Leyland in part exchange.

5   Also possibly numbered 6. New to D Davies, Abertridwr as a Ch25 body, rebodied B25 in 7/22. Probably withdrawn 6/30 and with A Hicks, Newport as a lorry by 9/31, last licensed /33.

6   Also possibly numbered 9. New to AJ Wilkins (Aberdare Motor Services) number 3, passing to Sirhowy Valley by 10/25 via John Norman, dealer, Cardiff. Withdrawn 9/27, sold 11/27 to owner in Newport, then Vite Brothers, Newport as lorry 5/28, last licensed 4/33.

7   This vehicle had pneumatic tyres on the front and solid on the rear. Withdrawn 12/29, disposal uncertain.

VEHICLES ACQUIRED FROM GRIFFIN MOTOR CO, 1926.

8	BO2100	Leyland 35hp			B26	/19
9	AX8060	AEC 202	202...		B26R	7/25
10	BO3036	Daimler CK			B26	/20
11	AX7674	Reo 25hp			B14	5/25
12	EU1640	Dennis		Hickman	B32	/22
13	EU2295	Dennis		Hickman?	B32	/25
14		Overland			Car	
15		Humber			Car	
16		Daimler			Chassis	
17		Daimler			Ch?	

GENERAL NOTES

(1) 12/13 were originally Griffin numbers 5 and 16. The other vehicles were acquired from the Blackwood (Mon) Motor Company in 12/25 and 8-11 were possibly numbered respectively 23, 22, 21 and 24 by Griffin.

(2) One Dennis was painted red and the other grey.

(3) One of the Daimlers may have been DU9931, Daimler CK, Ch26 body.

PARTICULAR NOTES BY VEHICLE NUMBER

8. Possibly originally registered by Leyland dealer in Cardiff. Withdrawn 12/29, possibly sold to Leyland in part exchange.

9. Also possibly numbered 12. Withdrawn 12/28, to Romilly Motors (dealer) Cardiff 6/29.

10. Also possibly numbered 7. Withdrawn 12/28 after crash at Pontllanfraith, dismantled and used for spares for 5 at about 3/30.

11. Withdrawn 6/27.

12. Withdrawn 12/28 at latest. Chassis may have been sold first.

13. Registered as a charabanc. Withdrawn 12/28 at latest. Chassis may have been sold first.

VEHICLES ACQUIRED FROM VALLEYS MOTOR BUS SERVICES, 1926

18	AX7017	Albion PH24		?	B21	1/25
19	AM8766	Commer RC	RC4367	SWCM	B30	11/20

PARTICULAR NOTES BY VEHICLE NUMBER

18. Remained on solid tyres with Board although there was a proposal to convert to pneumatics in 6/29. Withdrawn 12/29, to John Norman, Coachbuilders, Cardiff, 4/30.

19. New as an army lorry in 1917. To South Wales Commercial Motors Ltd (12) 9/21. To Hills, Tredegar 8/25 and towed from there to Blackwood. Withdrawn 10/26 and last licensed to Howells and Withers, Pontllanfraith, 4/30.

VEHICLE ACQUIRED FROM LEWIS & JAMES LTD, 1927

13	AX9617	Saurer 3AD	20030-38	Dodson	B30R	10/26

NOTES

This vehicle was purchased for the Bargoed Hill route but never actually operated by Lewis & James and sold to West Mon in 2/27. It was painted by W Meredith in 5/32. The livery was originally lavender blue, then orange and black, then maroon and cream. It was withdrawn 7/34 and broken up in early /35.

NEW VEHICLES, 1927

15	AX9947	Leyland PLSC3	45655	Leyland	B32R	3/27
16	AX9948	Leyland PLSC3	45656	Leyland	B32R	3/27
17	WO72	Leyland PLSC3	45448/6	Leyland	B32R	3/27
9	WO974	Saurer 3AD	20058/43	United	B32R	10/27

NOTES ON PARTICULAR VEHICLES

15. Later listed as 31-seater (8/39); withdrawn 4/39 and converted to ambulance for Monmouthshire CC by 5/40; returned to Board 1/46 and then sold.

16. Later listed as 31-seater; withdrawn by 10/39; ambulance as 15; to JH Lewis, dealer, Cardiff by 7/46.

17. This was a cancelled order by Green, Haverfordwest; withdrawn 1940 to become mobile casualty centre and to JH Lewis by 7/46; scrapped c1950.

9. In 11/30 it was minuted that there had been a partial collapse of the body and it was proposed that it be rebuilt or rebodied. In 7/39 it was converted to a breakdown lorry and ran on trade plates from 4/40. It appears from photographs of that period that it had been rebuilt or even rebodied and that it may have had a front entrance.

ACQUIRED VEHICLES, 1927

1	RP1541	Leyland C7	35643	Dodson	B28R	8/25
11	RP1542	Leyland C7	35642	Dodson	B28R	8/25
19	RP1543	Leyland C7	35641	Dodson	B28R	8/25
21	RP1544	Leyland C7	35645	Dodson	B28R	8/25
22	RP1545	Leyland C7	35644	Dodson	B28R	8/25

As this is the only known view of one of the ex-United Counties Leylands in service with West Mon, it is therefore included here for its rarity rather than its quality.

GENERAL NOTES

(1) These vehicles were originally owned by United Counties Omnibus Company Ltd and were numbered D2-6 by them.

(2) UCOC had sold D2/3 and also D1 (RP1540) to Regent Finance Co. Ltd, and were then sold on to the Board. However the receiver of Regent prevented the delivery of D1, which was later located at Parkhurst Garage, Holloway, London. The Board then agreed to buy D4-6 direct from UCOC. They all arrived in 10-12/27.

(3) All vehicles were withdrawn by West Mon in 1931.

PARTICULAR NOTES BY VEHICLE NUMBER

1. Disposal to Thomas & Evans (Corona), Porth, 5/31.
11. Disposal to Leyland 9/31 in part exchange.
19. Ditto. Then to Moore, Wombourn, /31 as goods vehicle.
21. Disposal as 1. Last licensed 12/36.
22. Disposal as 11. Then to Borough Engineer, Barking, /31 as Goods vehicle, last licensed 12/41.

NEW VEHICLES, 1929

| 2 | WO3238 | Leyland LT1 | 50589 | Leyland | B31D | 8/29 |
| 3 | WO3239 | Leyland LT1 | 50590 | Leyland | B31D | 8/29 |

GENERAL NOTES

(1) These vehicles were both converted with Leyland E54 oil engines in 1934.
(2) They are believed to be the first vehicles delivered in maroon and cream livery.

PARTICULAR NOTES BY VEHICLE NUMBER

2. Converted to B31R in 3/37. Body damaged in collision with Fair View Chapel, 1944. Withdrawn 8/47, to Hills, Tredegar, 11/47

3. Converted to B31R in 1/38. Withdrawn 9/47, to Hills 11/47, to T Evans, New Tredegar, 3/48, scrapped 1954.

ACQUIRED VEHICLE, 1929

| ? | ? | ADC 416D or Daimler | ? | ? | B.. | ? |

NOTES

This vehicle, of which details are scant, was purchased from a finance company in London and was in blue and cream livery. It was speedily returned when it was found to be stolen. There is also a reference to Leyland selling an old vehicle to the Board in 5/29, which may or may not be connected to this transaction.

NEW VEHICLES, 1930

4	WO4245	Leyland TS3	61234	Leyland	B29D	7/30
5	WO4246	Leyland TS3	61235	Leyland	B29D	7/30
1	WO4625	Leyland TQ1	66125	Dodson	B32D	9/30

PARTICULAR NOTES BY VEHICLE NUMBER

4. In 1/34 this vehicle was fitted with a Leyland E39 oil engine. It was converted to B32R in 3/37. Withdrawn 2/48, to W Harris, Argoed 5/48, Potter, Skewen 6/51, C Marshall, Nantyglo, last licensed /52. 4 and 5 were late arriving because of delays at Leyland and a Lion (7) was borrowed and later bought. In 2/43 it was reported that 4 was being prepared to be powered by producer gas at the HSG works at Treforest.

5. In 1934 this vehicle was fitted with a Leyland E39 oil engine. It was converted to B31R in 8/37. Withdrawn 4/47, and broken up.

1. This had a Leyland Bull Special 6 ton chassis. It was fitted with Leyland E39 oil engine in 10/34. In 2/48 it was withdrawn and the body removed by W Meredith, Rock and rebuilt before being fitted to the new 1. It had a handbrake on all 4 wheels of the 'push-on' type, a ratchet brake on the rear wheels, an engine throttle between clutch and foot brake, and a starter under the seat, so allowing the engine to be started with one foot on the throttle and one on the starter button. The footbrake worked on the rear wheels only.

ACQUIRED VEHICLE, 1930

| 7 | TE9373 | Leyland LT1 | 50278 | Leyland | B29R (?D) | 11/29 |

NOTES

This former demonstrator vehicle was borrowed from Leyland in 7/30 in blue and white livery to cover for the delay in delivery of 4 and 5. It was acquired in 10/30 and received a Leyland E54 oil engine in /34 and was reseated to 31 by 1/38: it may originally have had a dual entrance. It was withdrawn in 1/47 and scrapped by the Board in 4/47.

| 8 | WO5697 | Leyland LT3 | 51747 | Leyland | B32D | 9/31 |
| 10 | WO5913 | Leyland TQ3 | 67671 | Dodson | B30D | 12/31 |

In the above pictures both the Leylands have been rebodied by Burlingham.

GENERAL NOTES

Both these vehicles were purchased from Leyland in part exchange for 3 Leyland C7 vehicles as set out above. Originally the order was for 3 Leyland TS1s, then 2 TS1s, then for these two in lieu.

PARTICULAR NOTES BY VEHICLE NUMBER

8. Renumbered to 8A in 1953 when new 8 delivered. It was fitted with a Leyland oil engine by 7/33 and was converted to B36R in 5/38. It was rebodied by Burlingham B34F in 10/43 and the old body was noted with A Lewis 9/43 and in a field by /45. It was withdrawn in 2/54: disposal to C Morgan, Pengam 10/54 for scrap.

10. This was similar to the earlier Bull. It was fitted with a Leyland oil engine in 11/34 and received a new Burlingham B32F body in 8/46. It was withdrawn in 11/55 and gradually became derelict: the remains were scrapped by Bryn Motor Company, Pontllanfraith, in 3/58.

ACQUIRED VEHICLE, 1931

6	PL2223	Leyland KP1	4	Leyland	C20F	1/30

NOTES

This vehicle was termed by Leyland a 'proof' model, as one of the first Cubs. It was on demonstration to Green, Haverfordwest and offered to them in 11/30; it was offered to the Board who accepted it. It was sent to the Leyland factory at Kingston for repainting and alterations including a new door and entered service in 2/31. It was decorated for the Coronation in 1937 and withdrawn in 1939. It became a mobile casualty centre for Monmouthshire CC in 7/40 and passed to Pascoe, Pengam in 4/45.

ACQUIRED VEHICLES, 1932

| 12 | WO2209 | Thornycroft A20 Long | 15406 | Hall Lewis | B20D | 10/28 |
| 11 | WO2210 | Thornycroft A20 Long | 15407 | Hall Lewis | B20D | 10/28 |

GENERAL NOTES

These vehicles were acquired from Ralphs Garages, possibly as early as 5/32 after they had given up their service between Oakdale and Crumlin. They were numbered 31/2 by Ralphs. They were both overhauled in the Board workshops in 11/32 and entered service at least by 6/33.

PARTICULAR NOTES BY VEHICLE NUMBER

12. This is believed to have operated as a one man vehicle with the rear door closed. Withdrawn after mechanical failure 9/38, disposal not traced.
11. Withdrawn 5/35 after Abertysswg route suspended. Disposal to Bedwellty UDC for use as fire engine.

NEW VEHICLES, 1935

| 14 | WO9687 | Leyland TS6c | 5549 | Leyland | B32R | 4/35 |
| 13 | AAX27 | Leyland TSC9 | 5548 | Weymann | B32R | 8/35 |

PARTICULAR NOTES BY VEHICLE NUMBER

14. This was oil engined from delivery as were all subsequent vehicles. The torque converter was soon replaced. It was returned to Leyland for body modifications in 9/35 and 12/36. It was loaned to Caerphilly UDC in 4/44 after a fire. It was withdrawn 5/50 and to RI Davies, Tredegar, 8/50.

13. Body number W1013. This was a Leyland Alpine Beaver chassis modified as the Bulls but with an overdrive system. It was rebodied B32F by Burlingham in 1944-5. It was rebuilt by W Meredith, between 1/52 and 6/53 with sliding ventilators. It was withdrawn in 5/59 and in 6/59 was acquired by West of England Transport Collection, Winkleigh for preservation. In 1974 it passed to D Hoare, Chepstow and the body was scrapped by 1976. It was loaned to J Pettie, Edinburgh in 7/80 and restored as a replica of Alexander lorry 158, a TSC8 towing lorry.

NEW VEHICLE, 1937

18	CAX42	Leyland TS8c	16105	Willowbrook	B37F	12/37

NOTES

Body number 3049. This vehicle had its torque converter replaced and by 12/53 was reseated to B35F. Withdrawn 1/55 and to DMD Contractor, Birchgrove, Cardiff by 6/55.

ACQUIRED VEHICLE, 1937

11	BWK515	Daimler COG5/40	8226	Willowbrook	B39F	6/36

NOTES

Body number 2900. This vehicle was a former demonstrator and acquired from Daimler in 1/37 after being demonstrated to Rhondda Transport. By 9/52 it was fitted with sliding ventilators and in 8/53 it was renumbered to 11A. It was to be rebuilt by Meredith in 1/54 but in fact was withdrawn 1/54 and to DMD Contractor, Birchgrove, Cardiff by 4/54.

NEW VEHICLES, 1939

12	DAX 334	Leyland TS8c	302183	Willowbrook	B37F	5/39
16	DAX335	Leyland TS8c	302184	Willowbrook	B37F	5/39

12. Body number 3155. Later converted to crash gearbox. Rebuilt by Meredith 1951-2 and reseated to 35. Withdrawn 10/54 and to Rees, Llanelly Hill 11/54.

16. Body number 3156. Later converted to crash gearbox. Withdrawn 1955: to DMD Ltd, Birchgrove, Cardiff, 6/55.

ACQUIRED VEHICLE, 1940

| 19 | KMG484 | AEC Regal | 06623374 | Willowbrook | B37F | 4/39 |

NOTES

Body number 3213. This vehicle was on extended hire from AEC from 4/39 and acquired in 6/40. It had a preselective gearbox. It was withdrawn in 9/56 and to Bryn Motor Company, Pontllanfraith in 10/56.

NEW VEHICLES, 1941

| 6 | EAX728 | Daimler COG5 | 8493 | Weymann | B39F | 11/41 |
| 20 | EAX729 | Daimler COG6 | 11152 | Metro-Cammell | H32/26R | 11/41 |

PARTICULAR NOTES BY VEHICLE NUMBERS

6. Body number M2523. This vehicle was 8ft wide and 30ft long and was destined for Salisbury, Southern Rhodesia. It had sunblinds and silver foil in the roof to restrict heat. It had an OMO style cab nearside window, no driver's offside door, and initially no emergency exit (one was later fitted in the rear with the loss of one seat). It was delivered in a grey livery but later repainted. It was often used post war on the Cardiff service, but on the Pontypridd route it had to reverse at one point as the lock was insufficient. It was fitted with an AEC 6-cylinder engine in 1956, probably from 19 (KMG 484). It was withdrawn in 5/60, to Courtenay, Upper Trelyn 10/60 for scrap, but still there 4/63.

20. Body: contract 239. This was the first double deck vehicle in the fleet and was 8ft wide: it was

destined for Johannesburg and was in typical South African style with a route number box which was never used. It was restricted in its use because of its highbridge configuration. In 3/44 the chassis fractured and Daimler repaired it. Withdrawn 7/57, to Remplance, London E14 for scrap.

NEW VEHICLES, 1943

9	EWO364	Guy Arab I 5LW	FD25863	Strachan	L27/28R	4/43
22	EWO578	Daimler CWA6	11412	Duple	L27/28R	6/43
21	EWO579	Guy Arab II 5LW	FD25985	Massey	H30/26R	8/43

GENERAL NOTES

These vehicles were all to utility standards with wooden seats and were delivered in grey or brown but soon repainted.

PARTICULAR NOTES BY VEHICLE NUMBERS

9. It was later fitted with a Gardner 6LW engine. In 10/51 it was sent to Bruce for repairs but because of the demise of that firm it was sent to H Richards & Co between 12/51 and 9/52. It was withdrawn in 9/57 and passed to Remblance, London E14 11/57 for scrap.

22. Body number 37175. It was rebuilt by Romilly Motors, Cardiff between 9/55 and 1/56 with sliding ventilators and a one piece opening windscreen. Withdrawn 9/57, to Bell St Motors, Henley 11/57.

21. Body number C1419. It was out of service in 8/49 and used for demonstration to the police of lifting techniques of an overturned bus. It was rebodied by Bruce Coachworks, L27/26R, between 3/50 and 10/50 but kept its high radiator. Withdrawn 7/61, to Stevens and Sons, dealers, Gloucester, 1/62.

NEW VEHICLES, 1944

23	EWO858	Daimler CWA6	11599	Duple	L27/26R	3/44
24	EWO896	Daimler CWA6	11729	Brush	L27/28R	5/44
25	EWO895	Daimler CWA6	11718	Brush	L27/28R	6/44

GENERAL NOTES

These were all delivered to utility specifications, similar to the 1943 deliveries. All lost their upper deck front ventilators when rebuilt.

PARTICULAR NOTES BY VEHICLE NUMBERS

23.   Body number: 37200. This was rebuilt with rubber mounted windows by Romilly Motors, Cardiff between 7/53 and 1/54. Withdrawn 5/58, derelict for some time, to AGH Jordan, Blaenavon, for spares, 4/59.

24.   This was rebuilt by Romilly Motors c1956 and was reseated to L27/26R. Withdrawn 3/60, to

Courtenay, Upper Trelyn for scrap 10/60.

25. This was not fully rebuilt but received some rubber mounted windows. Withdrawn 10/57, to Bell St. Motor Works, Henley, 11/57, then to Northampton Corporation by 8/59 as a tar wagon.

ACQUIRED VEHICLES, 1945

| 26 | YG7449 | Leyland TS6 | 4871 | Burlingham | B32F | 5/34 |
| 27 | HB5948 | Bedford OWB | 8503 | Duple | B32F | 8/42 |

GENERAL NOTES

These vehicles were acquired on 1/11/45 with the business of Jones Brothers (Treharris) Ltd (trading as Commercial Motor Services) and were formerly numbered 9 and 16 respectively.

PARTICULAR NOTES BY VEHICLE NUMBERS

26. This was new to Ripponden & District, passing to Jones in 12/35: it was rebodied by Burlingham in 2/45. Withdrawn 4/48 and passed to RI Davies, Tredegar: withdrawn by them 7/55 and to South Wales Motor Traders, Newport.

27. Body number 31669. This vehicle gave a great deal of trouble. It was repainted in Board livery and it is believed that its wooden seats were replaced by upholstered seats from 14 and 17. It was out of service by 1/50, withdrawn 4/50 and scrapped by Morgan, Pengam in that month.

NEW VEHICLES, 1947

15	FWO747	Leyland PD1	462542	Leyland	L27/26R	4/47
5	GAX671	Leyland PS1	471360	Willowbrook	B35F	8/47
7	GAX672	Leyland PS1	471361	Willowbrook	B35F	8/47
2	GAX846	Daimler CVD6	13311	Willowbrook	B35F	10/47
3	GAX847	Daimler CVD6	13312	Willowbrook	B35F	10/47

PARTICULAR NOTES BY VEHICLE NUMBERS

15. This was fitted with a push out ventilator on the nearside upper deck window in 1950. It also had its waistband brought round blow windscreen towards the end of its life. It was withdrawn 5/63 and disposed of in 8/65 to Courtenay, Upper Trelyn for scrap.

5. Body number 6259. Rebuilt between 1/ and 8/60. Withdrawn 8/63, to Courtenay for scrap 3/64.

7. Body number 6260. Rebuilt between 5/ and 11/58 and 8/60 and 6/61. Withdrawn 12/63, to Courtney for scrap 3/64.

2. Body number 6285. This and 3 were regarded as very slow. Rebuilt 3/59 and 7/60. Withdrawn 5/61, to Stevens & Sons, Gloucester for scrap 1/62.

3. Body number 6286. Rebuilt 9/55 to 5/56 by Meredith. Withdrawn 6/61, to Stevens for scrap 1/62.

NEW VEHICLES, 1948

17	GWO422	AEC Regent III	0961884	Massey	L27/26R	4/48
26	GWO521	Leyland PD2/1	481045	Leyland	L27/26R	4/48
4	GWO522	Leyland PD2/1	481044	Leyland	L27/26R	4/48

PARTICULAR NOTES BY VEHICLE NUMBERS

17.   This was rebuilt by the Board between 11/52 and 5/53 and completely rebuilt again by the Board between 5/62 and 7/63, including, it is thought, a new roof. Consideration was given to taking the body off Guy 17 and placing it on this vehicle. It was withdrawn 4/65 and the engine used for 29. The remainder went to Courtenay, Upper Trelyn, for scrap 2/66.

26.   This and 4 had the cream waistband brought under the windscreen in later years. Withdrawn by 4/70 and to Telefilms Transport, Preston.

4.   This acquired some rubber mounted windows. Withdrawal and disposal as 26.

NEW VEHICLES, 1949

28	HWO189	AEC Regent III	9612E2641	Bruce	L27/26R	6/49
29	HWO190	AEC Regent III	9612E2642	Bruce	L27/26R	6/49
1	HWO590	Foden PVSC6	26680	Dodson	B31R	7/49

PARTICULAR NOTES BY VEHICLE NUMBERS

28.   The bodywork was by Bruce on East Lancs frames and was numbered 4444. This and 29 were completed at the same time as vehicles for Gellygaer UDC and Green, Haverfordwest. This vehicle had a bad accident in Blackwood and was off the road for this and/or rebuilding in 4-8/58 (carried out by Meredith) and from 7-12/62. The waistband was brought round beneath the windscreen, as was 29. It was withdrawn 9/66 and to Courtenay, Upper Trelyn for scrap 12/66.

29.   Body as above, number 4445. This vehicle was in a serious accident at Cilfynydd and was off road 1/63 to 5/64 for rebuilding. It ended up with rubber mounted front upper deck windows, first and last upper deck side windows and front indicator glass. In 1966 it was fitted with the engine from 17. Withdrawn 11/67, to Courtenay for scrap 2/68.

1.   The chassis of this was completed by 2/48 and it then received the Dodson body from the previous 1 (WO4625) which was withdrawn that month. The transfer was carried out by Meredith, retaining the elliptical rear window but fitting new sliding windows and removing the front entrance. It had a ratchet type rear brake operating on the outside of the rear brake

drums which came on automatically in the event of a faulty gear change when ascending Bargoed Hill. The Traffic Commissioners insisted on the fitting of a small motor pump to the braking system, operated by a toggle switch if the engine failed. There were problems with the braking system throughout. A new Willowbrook B31F body (52086) was fitted between 10/52 and 2/53. It was withdrawn in 3/65 and sold for scrap 8/65.

Photographs of the 1930 Dodson body after transfer to HWO 590, showing the distinctive rear elliptical window, are rare thus justifying the inclusion of this less than perfect image.

NEW VEHICLES, 1950

14	JAX480	Daimler CVD6	16784	Bruce	L27/26R	5/50
27	JAX500	Daimler CVD6	16785	Bruce	L27/26R	5/50

PARTICULAR NOTES BY VEHICLE NUMBERS

14. The bodywork was by Bruce on East Lancs frames (4620). This vehicle had its livery modified later with the cream band beneath the windscreen. It was withdrawn 3/62, and kept in reserve until passing to Courtenay, Upper Trelyn for scrap 6/63.

27. Bodywork (4629) and livery change as per 14. Withdrawn 5/62 and kept in reserve until disposal as per 14.

NEW VEHICLE, 1952

30	KWO368	Foden PVSC6	32260	Willowbrook	B31F	6/52

NOTES

This body (52999) was different in detail from the new body fitted a few months later to Foden 1. A cream band under the windscreen was added later. The braking system was similar to 1, and like it there were always problems since the gearing was so low that they had to be driven down Bargoed Hill. They were used otherwise only on the Wyllie route. It was extremely noisy and could be heard up to a mile away. Withdrawn 4/65 after an accident in Bedwellty Road and to Courtenay, Upper Trelyn for scrap.

NEW VEHICLES, 1953-4

8	LWO322	Leyland PD2/12	531572	Leyland	L27/26R	8/53
11	LWO323	Leyland PD2/12	531525	Leyland	L27/26R	8/53
12	MWO389	Leyland PD2/12	541228	Leyland	L27/26R	9/54

GENERAL NOTES

These were the first post-war 8ft wide vehicles in the fleet and were delivered in a revised livery of maroon with cream window frames. They were repainted in 3 band livery and later the lower cream band was brought round under the front cab window.

PARTICULAR NOTES BY VEHICLE NUMBERS

8. Fitted with trafficators by 2/63. Withdrawn by 6/71 and to Way, Cardiff for scrap 9/72.
11. Also fitted with trafficators. Withdrawn 5/68 and to Mullins, Pengam for scrap 9/68.
12. Renumbered 12A in 12/68. Withdrawn 2/69, to Mullins, Pengam for scrap 4/69.

NEW VEHICLE, 1955

18	MWO709	Leyland PSUC1/1	544787	Weymann	B44F	1/55

NOTES

This was the first underfloor engine vehicle in the fleet. It was delivered in maroon with cream window surrounds and later painted with one cream band. By 2/63 it had trafficators. By 6/71 it was in blue livery. It was withdrawn in 1972 for use as a trainer and was derelict by 2/77: to Wigley, dealer, Carlton for scrap 7/78.

ACQUIRED VEHICLE, 1955

16	168DMU	AEC Monocoach	MC3RV053	Willowbrook	B45F	1/55

NOTES

The bodywork was by Willowbrook (54195) on Park Royal frames (37305). The vehicle was exhibited in shell form at the 1954 Commercial Motor Show and was demonstrated to Western Welsh after completion. It was acquired by the Board from AEC in 5/55. It had a white or cream livery as a demonstrator and was repainted by the Board in the cream window livery before later being modified. The brightwork on the front and side was removed over the years. It was returned to AEC for a lower ratio differential to be fitted. It was withdrawn in 5/67 and passed to Howells and Withers, Pontllanfraith.

NEW VEHICLES, 1956

10	PWO479	AEC Reliance	MU3RA509	Willowbrook	B43F	9/56
19	PWO480	AEC Reliance	MU3RA510	Willowbrook	B43F	9/56

PARTICULAR NOTES BY VEHICLE NUMBERS

10. Body number 56807. These vehicles had AH470 engines and suffered head gasket and half shaft problems. Trafficators were later fitted. Withdrawn 11/68 and to Howells and Withers, Pontllanfraith, then to EI Peake, Pontnewynydd by 6/69.

19. Body number 56808. Withdrawn /68; to Cowley, dealer, Salford, then RI Davies, Tredegar 2/69, WT Edwards, Lydbrook 10/69; to Wyatt and Tizard, Birmingham, 6/75.

NEW VEHICLES, 1957-8

9	SAX186	Leyland PD2/40	571959	Willowbrook	L27/28RD	9/57
22	SAX187	Leyland PD2/40	571960	Willowbrook	L27/28RD	10/57
25	SAX188	Leyland PD2/40	571961	Willowbrook	L27/28RD	10/57
23	TAX710	Leyland PD2/40	581001	Willowbrook	L27/28RD	6/58

GENERAL NOTES

These vehicles were the first in the fleet with platform doors, heaters and a sliding drivers' door. They had push out ventilators on the front upper deck and destination indicators over the platform. When new they had a three cream band livery with a narrow centre band.

At various times, the four Willowbrook double-deck bodies in the fleet carried a variety of styles of application of the maroon and cream livery, as may be seen on this and the opposite page.

PARTICULAR NOTES BY VEHICLE NUMBER

9. Body number 57966. Repainted by Caerphilly UDC 4/71. Withdrawn 1972, sold for preservation, to Hunt, Isle of Wight by 10/86.

22. Body number 57967. In blue livery by 6/71. Withdrawn 10/73 and remained derelict at depot.

25. Body number 57968. In blue livery by 70-1. Withdrawn 10/73 and dismantled and sold for spares 12/73.

23. Body number 58065. In 1/59 this vehicle was in an accident at Caerphilly and was repaired by Willowbrook over 3 months. In blue livery by 6/73. To Islwyn.

ACQUIRED VEHICLE, 1957

20	NLP635	AEC Monocoach	U163473	Park Royal	B45F	6/53

NOTES

Body number B36803. This was the prototype Monocoach and weighed less than the Reliances despite having a preselective/epicyclic gearbox. Its frontal appearance differed from production examples and it had a manually operated folding entrance door. It was extensively demonstrated to LT, from 7/53 to 4/54 in dark green livery with Green Line transfers on 447 and later 711 at Reigate, then from 1/54 at Dalston on 208/208A with LT fleetnames. In 8/55 it was demonstrated to Glasgow. In 1/56 it was back with LT at Reigate until 3/57. In 5/57 it was demonstrated to the Board which bought it for £2711 in 8/57. It was still in green livery until repainted in one banded Board livery: the LT style wheel trims were removed and in due course trafficators were fitted and the front chromium strips were painted over. It was withdrawn by 5/67 and passed to Howells and withers, Pontllanfraith. By 3/68 it was in a scrap yard at Amblecote.

13	UWO688	Leyland PD2/38	583400	Willowbrook	B31F	3/59

NOTES

Body number 59179. This unique vehicle was 7ft 6ins wide with a cut off rear end and sprag brakes. As new it rode very harshly and the springs were replaced by those from a PS1 to improve this. After Bargoed Hill was bypassed, the body was removed and the chassis widened by the Board to 8ft and a new engine, gearbox and differential was fitted. It was then sent to Massey for a new body (2680), L27/28RD, in 6/66. This had a fixed windscreen and long handle for the front indicator. In 11/69 it was the first double decker repainted into blue and had a non-standard livery shared with 11, in which there was more white than standard. It was transferred to Islwyn.

NEW VEHICLES, 1960

6	XWO342	Leyland PSUC1/11	604375	Willowbrook	B45F	5/60
24	XWO473	Leyland PD2/40	592830	Longwell Green	L27/28RD	5/60

PARTICULAR NOTES BY VEHICLE NUMBER

6.   Body number 59562. This was the first single deck vehicle to be repainted in blue (11/69). It was fitted with a 0400 engine later, and had a large destination indicator that was blanked off. It was withdrawn in 6/73 and dismantled for spares in 12/73 and the body removed.

24.   Body number 17994. This vehicle had a narrow cream band when new above the lower deck windows. It was withdrawn in /71 after an accident and later cannibalised for spares.

NEW VEHICLES, 1961

2	125BAX	Leyland PSUC1/11	607685	Weymann	B45F	5/61
3	126BAX	Leyland PSUC1/11	607686	Weymann	B45F	5/61
21	260BAX	Leyland PD2/40	592830	Massey	L27/28RD	6/61

PARTICULAR NOTES BY VEHICLE NUMBERS

2, 3. Body numbers M9752/3. They were later fitted with 0400 engines. They had Olympic style mouldings on the sides as supplied to Edinburgh Corporation. Both passed to Islwyn.

21. Body number 2436. This had a long operating handle to the front destination blind. On 31/7/67 this vehicle went down an embankment at Pontllanfraith and was repaired by the Board over 11 months. To Islwyn.

NEW VEHICLES, 1962

14	203CWO	Leyland PD2/40	613249	Massey	L27/28RD	3/62
27	204CWO	Leyland PD2/40	613250	Massey	L27/28RD	3/62
19	296FAX	Commer 1500	22538	Rootes	C11	11/62

PARTICULAR NOTES BY VEHICLE NUMBERS

14. Body number 2472. Repainted in new livery by 6/73. Operating handle as 21. This vehicle and 27 had formica seat backs and staggered upstairs seating. To Islwyn.
27. Body number 2471. Otherwise as per 14.
19. Supplied by Bufton. Withdrawn 6/69 and to Trelyn Metals 8/69.

NEW VEHICLES, 1963-4

5	404HAX	Leyland PSUC1/11	L10261	Willowbrook	B45F	8/63
7	405HAX	Leyland PSUC1/11	L10260	Willowbrook	B45F	8/63
1	AWO528B	Leyland PSUC1/11	L30725	Willowbrook	B45F	8/64
30	AWO532B	Leyland PSUC1/11	L30726	Willowbrook	B45F	8/64

NOTES

Body numbers CF624/5, 866/7 respectively. These were old style BET bodies. They were repainted as follows: 1 by 4/70, 5 and 7 by 6/71 and 30 by 6/73. All to Islwyn.

NEW VEHICLES, 1965-6

15	EWO195C	Leyland PD2/40	L24300	Massey	L27/28RD	4/65
17	GWO351C	Leyland PD2/40	L41695	Massey	L27/28RD	12/65
28	KWO134D	Leyland PD2/40	L61971	Massey	L27/28RD	12/66

PARTICULAR NOTES BY VEHICLE NUMBERS

15. Body number 2633. Long operating handle to destination blind and opening windscreen. In new livery by 6/73. To Islwyn.
17. Body number 2649. As 15 but with fixed windscreen and in new livery by 6/71.
28. Body number 2691. Last new double decker, as 17. Painted in new livery 5/70 with more blue, which became standard.

ACQUIRED VEHICLES, 1967

| 16 | JBO117 | Leyland PSUC1/1 | 543558 | Weymann | B44F | 10/54 |
| 20 | JBO118 | Leyland PSUC1/1 | 543557 | Weymann | B44F | 10/54 |

GENERAL NOTES

These vehicles came from Western Welsh in 5/67. They were later fitted for one man operation.

PARTICULAR NOTES BY VEHICLE NUMBERS

16. Body number M6545. Previously at Cross Keys depot. One of these had a 0400 engine fitted. Withdrawn 1972 and nominally scrapped 2/72 but derelict until to Way, Cardiff, for scrap 7/73.
20. Body number M6539. Previously at Cwmbran depot. In 3/71, 10 was out of service and the engine was fitted to 20. Withdrawn 1972 and nominally scrapped 11/72 but derelict until to Way, Cardiff, for scrap 7/73.

NEW VEHICLE, 1968

29	OAX160F	Leyland PSU4/1R	702969	Willowbrook	B45F	2/68

NOTES

Body number CF1614. This vehicle had a BET style pre-curved screen design. It was repainted to new livery by 6/71 and to Islwyn.

ACQUIRED VEHICLES, 1968

11	UNN111	Leyland PD2/21	556396	Metro-Cammell	L31/28RD	6/56
12	UNN115	Leyland PD2/20	556322	Metro-Cammell	L31/28RD	12/56
10	FCH19	Leyland PSUC1/1	534807	Saro	B44F	/54

PARTICULAR NOTES BY VEHICLE NUMBERS

11.　Formerly East Midland D111: to Cowley, dealer, Salford, 6/68, to Board 7/68. New Look front and air brakes. Repainted as 13 by 6/71 and withdrawn 2/72, to Way, Cardiff for scrap 9/72.

12.　Formerly East Midland D115: to Cowley, dealer, Salford, 6/68, to Board 11/68. New Look front and vacuum brakes. Withdrawn 1/70 and to Telefilms Transport, Preston minus engine 4/70.

10.　Body number 1562. Formerly Trent 369, to RI Davies, Tredegar, 11/65 and to Board 12/68. It was the last vehicle in the old livery and never repainted. Out of service by 3/71 and to Way, Cardiff for scrap 9/72.

NEW VEHICLE, 1969

| 19 | UAX222H | BMC 250JU | 20889 | BMC | C12 | 10/69 |

NOTES

This vehicle inaugurated the new livery. It was a PSV but lost its fleet number in 1970. To Islwyn.

NEW VEHICLES, 1970-3

4	VAX62H	Leyland PSU4A/2R	903934	Willowbrook	B47F	3/70
12	VAX63H	Leyland PSU4A/2R	903935	Willowbrook	B47F	3/70
19	VAX64H	Leyland PSU4A/2R	903936	Willowbrook	B47F	3/70
8	YAX993J	Leyland PSU3A/2R	7004553	Willowbrook	B53F	5/71
10	YAX994J	Leyland PSU3A/2R	7004554	Willowbrook	B53F	5/71
26	YAX995J	Leyland PSU3A/2R	700555	Willowbrook	B53F	5/71
11	CAX764K	Leyland PSU3B/2R	7303934	Willowbrook	B47F	2/72
16	CAX765K	Leyland PSU3B/2R	7303935	Willowbrook	B47F	2/72
24	CAX766K	Leyland PSU3B/2R	7303936	Willowbrook	B47F	2/72
9	GAX568L	Leyland PSUB3/2R	7203146	Willowbrook	B53F	/72
18	GAX569L	Leyland PSUB3/2R	7203147	Willowbrook	B53F	/72
20	GAX570L	Leyland PSUB3/2R	7203148	Willowbrook	B53F	/72
6	OAX972M	Leyland PSU4B/2R	7303934	Willowbrook	B45F	11/73
22	OAX973M	Leyland PSU4B/2R	7303935	Willowbrook	B45F	11/73
25	OAX974M	Leyland PSU4B/2R	730936	Willowbrook	B45F	11/73

NOTES

VAX batch were body numbers CF2005-7: they had BET windscreens and fixed side windows with 'roof lights' and were the first full sized vehicles delivered in the blue livery.

YAX batch were body numbers CF2316-8 which had similar side windows and lights. They were the first 36ft long vehicles in the fleet.

CAX batch were body numbers 71019-21, and GAX batch 72305-7: all were 36ft long and had similar side windows and lights.

OAX batch were body numbers 72375-7 and had hopper type ventilators and PAYE indicators. They were of 33ft length.

All vehicles passed to Islwyn.

A selection of the fifteen Leopards delivered between 1970-73 is shown on the following pages.

1970

1971

The 1971 deliveries were the first 36ft vehicles in the fleet and were followed in early 1972 by three more Leopards.

1972

1972 saw two batches of Leopards arrive; three in spring and three in autumn.

The final 1972 Leyland deliveries were 36ft long whereas the final vehicles purchased by the Board in 1973 reverted to not only to 33ft, but also had opening side windows.

1973

A fully-detailed and splendidly-illustrated history of the Pemberton based

MASSEY BROTHERS

coachbuilding activities is in preparation

Contact MDS Book Sales for free illustrated transport book/DVD catalogue.

128 Pikes Lane Glossop SK13 8EH

☎ 01457 861508

www.mdsbooks.co.uk

enquiries@mdsbooks.co,uk